Art of Celebration
COLORADO

INSPIRATION AND IDEAS FROM TOP EVENT PROFESSIONALS

Published by

PANACHE
PANACHE PARTNERS

Panache Partners, LLC
1424 Gables Court
Plano, TX 75075
469.246.6060
Fax: 469.246.6062
www.panache.com

Publishers: Brian G. Carabet and John A. Shand

Copyright © 2013 by Panache Partners, LLC
All rights reserved.

No part of this book may be reproduced or transmitted in any form or by any means, electronic or mechanical, including photocopying, recording, or by any information storage or retrieval system, except brief excerpts for the purpose of review, without written permission of the publisher.

All images in this book have been reproduced with the knowledge and prior consent of the professionals concerned and no responsibility is accepted by the producer, publisher, or printer for any infringement of copyright or otherwise arising from the contents of this publication. Every effort has been made to ensure that credits accurately comply with the information supplied.

Printed in Malaysia

Distributed by Independent Publishers Group
800.888.4741

PUBLISHER'S DATA

Art of Celebration Colorado

Library of Congress Control Number: 2012945529

ISBN 13: 978-0-9832398-8-8
ISBN 10: 0-9832398-8-6

First Printing 2013

10 9 8 7 6 5 4 3 2 1

This publication is intended to showcase the work of extremely talented people. The publisher does not require, warrant, endorse, or verify any professional accreditations, educational backgrounds, or professional affiliations of the individuals or firms included herein. All copy and photography published herein has been reviewed and approved as free of any usage fees or rights and accurate by the individuals and/or firms included herein.

Panache Partners, LLC, is dedicated to the restoration and conservation of the environment. Our books are manufactured with strict adherence to an environmental management system in accordance with ISO 14001 standards, including the use of paper from mills certified to derive their products from well-managed forests. We are committed to continued investigation of alternative paper products and environmentally responsible manufacturing processes to ensure the preservation of our fragile planet.

Art of Celebration
COLORADO

"Every detail, from the receipt of the invitations to the event itself, will set the mood for the celebration."
—Heather Allen

INTRODUCTION

Celebrations are woven into our lives from the moment we are born; we pave our long and winding road with revelry. Cultures are identified by their milestones, rites of passage, and faiths. From the visions of a select few, through the work of many, and motivated by all, our celebrations are universal.

In *Art of Celebration Colorado* we chart Colorado's modern-day visionaries who mastermind remarkable events, creating everlasting memories.

The magic of a phenomenal celebration is achieved with great collaboration. This book will take you on a journey, sharing the insights and creations of the gifted. We begin this journey with event planners—the directors and producers—who pull it all together, manage, and execute the visions even Before the Music Begins. And because once you've set the date, the next step is Location, Location, Location, we turn our focus to Colorado's most incredible venues, which become inspirational backdrops.

The event, floral, and lighting designers are true visionaries of Creating an Ambience; these artists are responsible for the endless ideas and boundless efforts and are often the heart and soul of an unforgettable gala. From there, It's All in the Details. Through the amazing talents of musicians, entertainers, photographers, and videographers, Capturing the Moment will forever keep alive the experiences of life's ritual—the art of celebration.

Art of Celebration Colorado will inspire, inform, and just might take your breath away!

Before the Music Begins

Table 6 Productions 14
Affair with Flair 26
Amy Toltz-Miller Special Events 36
Creative Events and Occasions 46
A Beautiful Memory 56
Calluna Events 64
Faye Gardenswartz 72
Frosted Pink Weddings 80
Special Events Design and Calligraphy 88
John Tobey Event Design 96
Kelli Kindel Events 102
Puttin' on the Ritz 108
WM Events 114

Location, Location, Location

Sanctuary 120
Della Terra Mountain Chateau 132
Aspen Meadows Resort 138
JW Marriott Denver Cherry Creek 142
The Little Nell 146
Palazzo Verdi 150
Seawell Grand Ballroom 154

CONTENTS

Creating an Ambience

DesignWorks by Dave and Mike 160
Newberry Brothers 172
The Aspen Branch 180
Bethel Party Rentals 186
Linens Unlimited 190
LMD Productions 194
Swank Stems 198

It's All in the Details

Elegant Bakery 204
JS Design 208
Signed & Sealed by Steph 212

Capturing the Moment

Andrew Clark Photography 218
Frances Photography 224
Studio JK 230
Autumn Burke Photography 236
BroxtonArt 240
Eric Stephenson Photography 244
Jared Wilson Photography 248
Lynda Hanshaw Photography 252
WonderWorks Studios 256

"Planning a party should be just as much fun as the party itself."
—William Fogler

Before the

TABLE 6 PRODUCTIONS

HEATHER ALLEN

Heather Allen didn't set out to make a career as an event planner, but when she and Table 6 Productions co-founder Shannon Wilson found themselves sitting at a disorganized, relatively prosaic wedding—at table number 6—the idea for their event planning firm was born. Specializing in everything from grand destination weddings to elegant, intimate affairs, "The 6 Chicks" team is ready to take a hands-on approach to event design and planning.

A "type A" personality, Heather is constantly on the go and imagining new ways of doing things—she's not one to copy the latest trends. Instead her events are custom, timeless, and a wonderful expression of her hosts' personalities. Forever accompanied by her two best friends—her MacBook and iPhone—Heather has been known to work well into the night or in the hours before dawn to bring a celebration from imagination to life. She is even known to actually dream up her next concept.

With offices throughout the United States, Table 6 is regularly featured on top wedding blogs and in magazines including *The Knot*, which ranked the firm's events among its best weddings from 2008 to 2011. Heather was honored as the event planner of the year at the 2011 Event Solutions Spotlight Awards, but all accolades aside, Heather and the rest of the Table 6 team remain passionate about providing hosts with one-of-a-kind events that will stay in their memories for years to come.

Snowflakes, proper lighting, crystals, glass, mirrored surfaces, and acrylic create an indoor winter wonderland for a couple with the last name Snow. Contrasted against flowers and linens in various creamy tones alongside the bling, the blue lights create an icy atmosphere; everything in the room absolutely shimmers.

Event Planning | 15

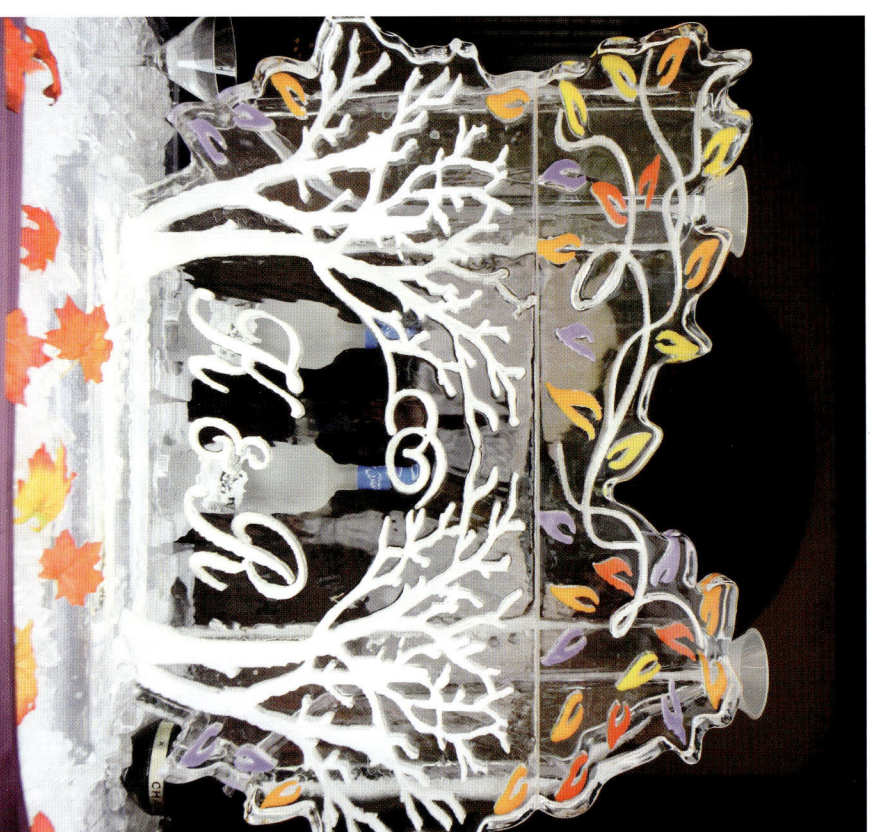

Photograph by Jenna Walker

Decor should complement the space, but it shouldn't get in the way of the guests. Candlelit lanterns, curtains of fall leaves, and tall centerpieces fill the open space above tables but don't obstruct conversation. Monograms are still a classic, personal way to celebrate a new union and can be designed to fit the couple's theme or personality.

"Everything about an event should reflect the hosts; it's their party."

—Heather Allen

"A touch of whimsy helps participants relax and enjoy themselves."
—Heather Allen

Photograph by broxtonArt

Photograph by broxtonArt

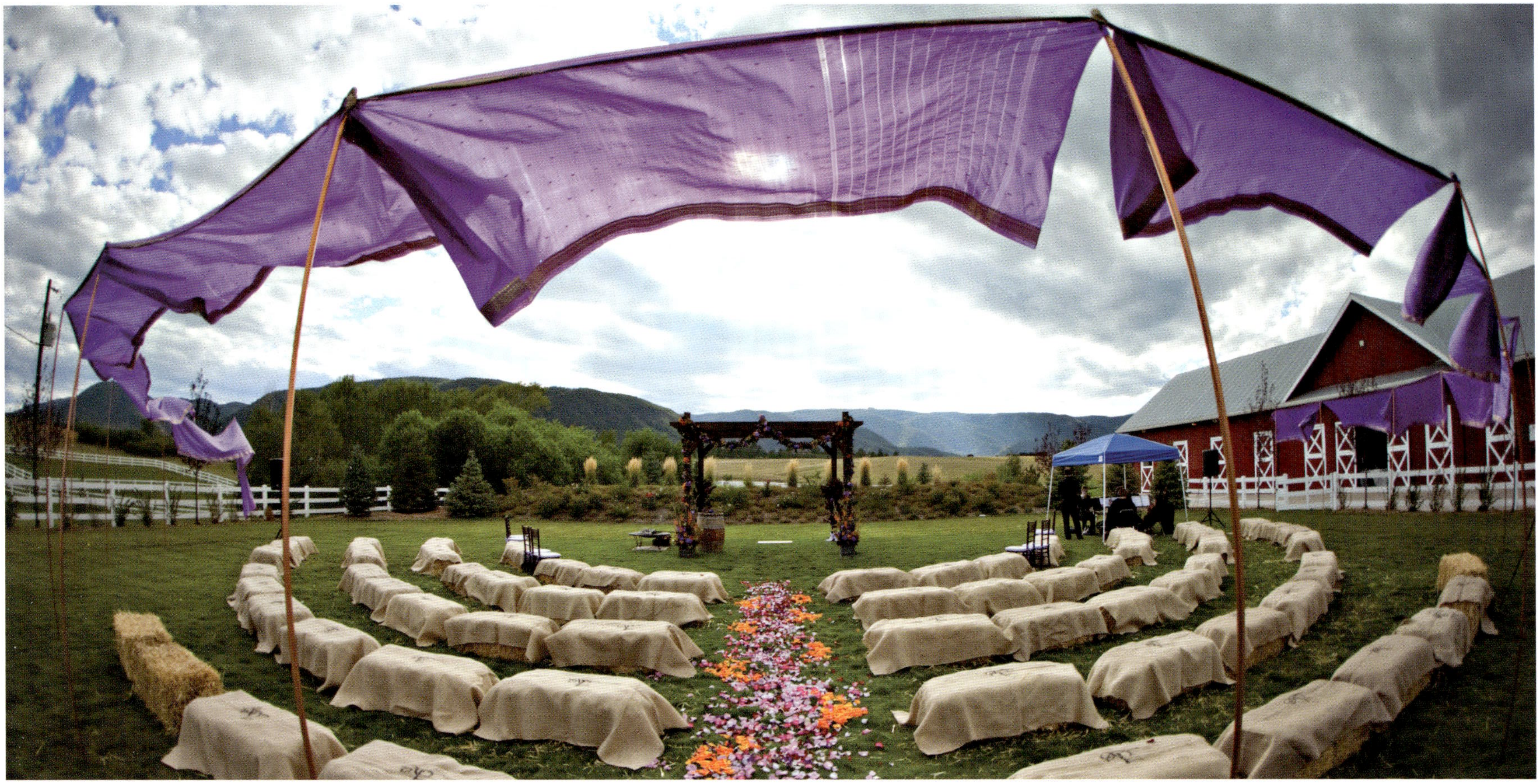

Photograph by broxtonArt

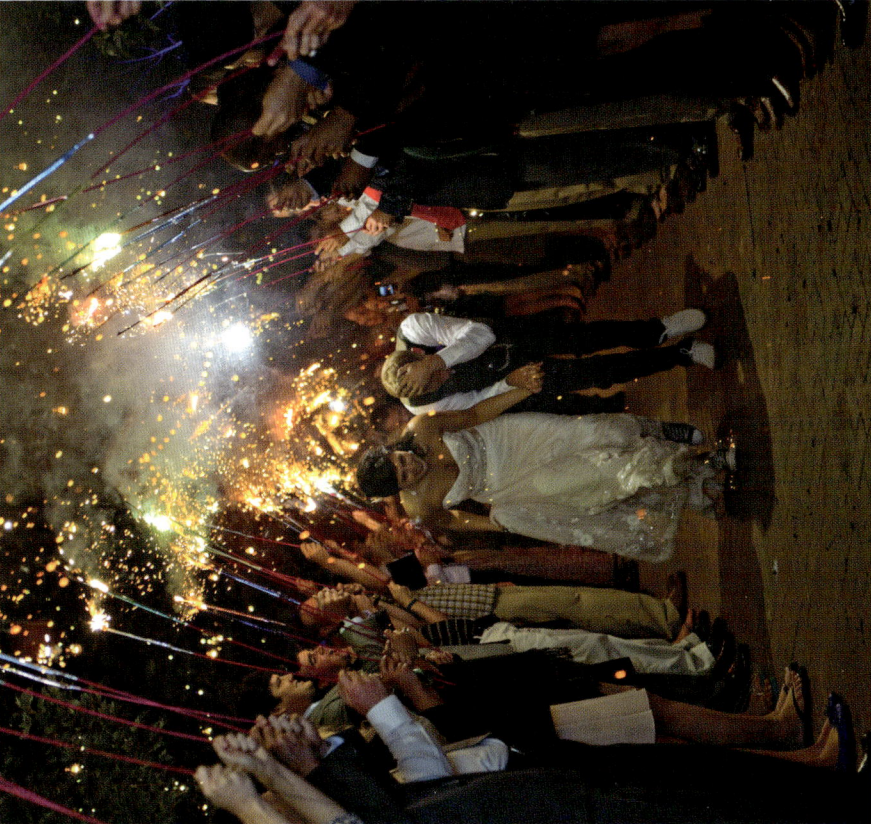

Years later, it's the unique details that people remember. Whether it's a clever piece of attire, a dining room that looks like a forest, unique ceremony seating, or fireworks during the bride and groom's getaway, the unexpected elements make a lasting impression.

Photograph by broxtonArt

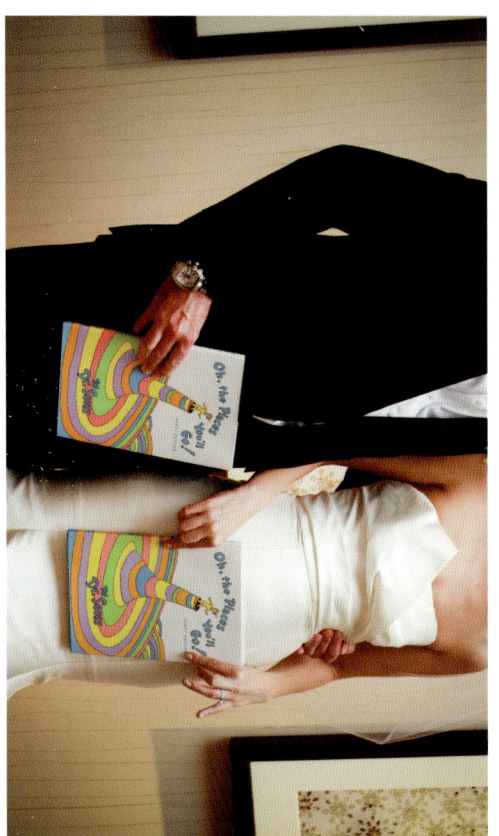

"It's your day, your way. It should be mahhhling dahhhling!" —Heather Allen

It's easy to overdo a wedding reception; if the visual details are pushed too far, an elegant design becomes oppressive. I like to keep lush settings to a conservative color scheme while adding fun, personal touches, like personalized copies of Dr. Seuss' *Oh, the Places You'll Go!* set on every chair so as not to obstruct the gorgeous elegance of the tablescape.

Art of Celebration | 22

Photograph by Nadia D Photography

Photograph by Nadia D Photography

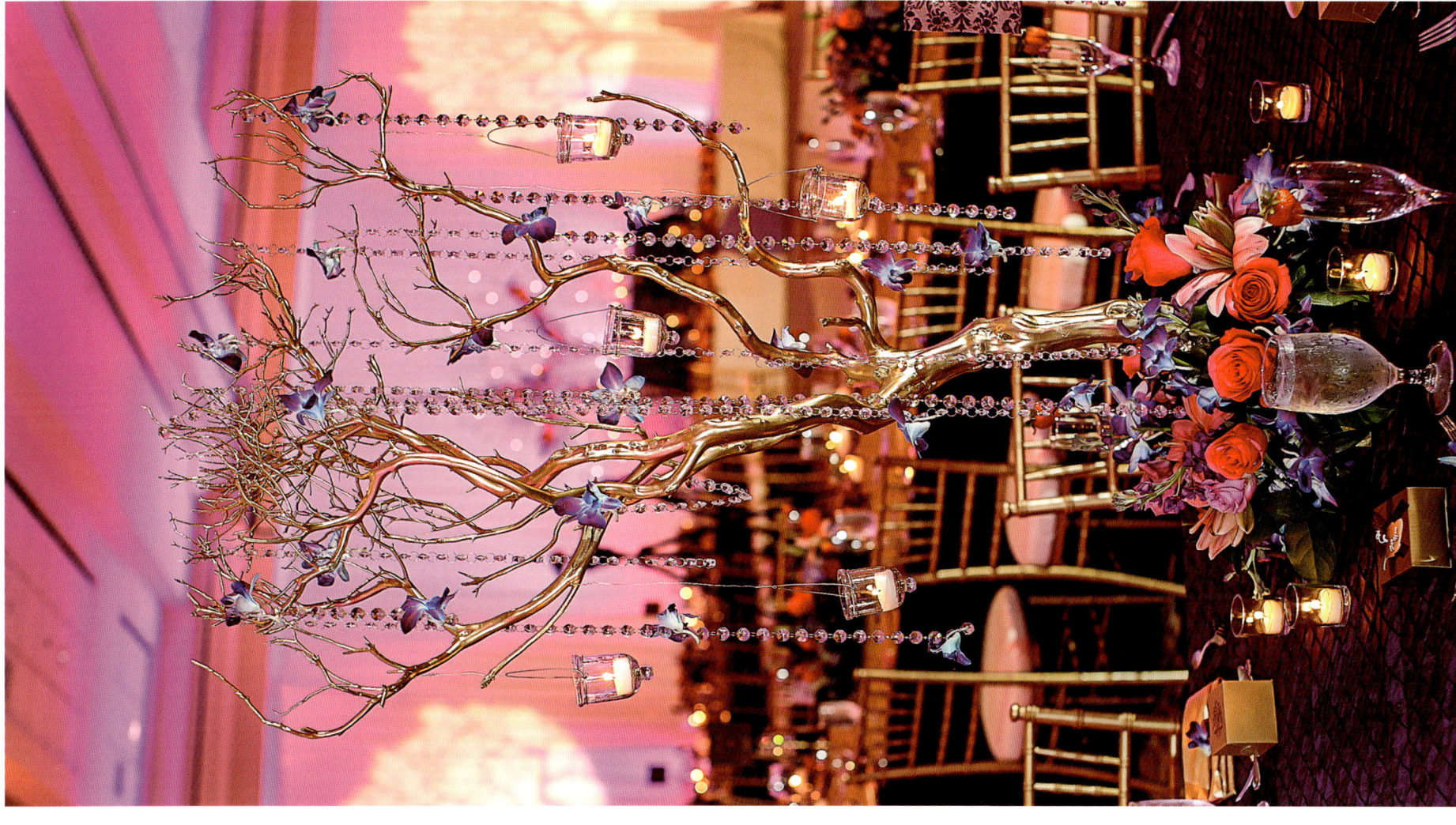

"If a host is relaxed, guests will be relaxed, and everyone will enjoy the event even more." —Heather Allen

Truly personal elements—how the couple met, references to an inside joke, or an element that has special meaning to the host—make the event more special and unlike any other. This is our goal when designing our events.

Art of Celebration | 24

Photograph by Frances Photography

Photograph by Frances Photography

Photograph by Frances Photography

"Every detail, from the receipt of the invitations to the event itself, will set the mood for the celebration."
—Heather Allen

Like the invitations sent out weeks before an event, color and lighting help define the tone of an evening. Pops of brilliant hot pink or royal blue against pleats of fabric heighten the glamour and provide a colorful backdrop for the party.

views

Find an event planner who is your advocate in every way, someone who will hold your hand when you need it and will represent your best interests when meeting with vendors.

AFFAIR WITH FLAIR

LISA COOK | LESLIE HEINS

It's a standard assumption that the goal of all event architects is to create a memorable experience. Since 1982, Lisa Cook and Leslie Heins, the owners of Affair with Flair, have partnered to help their clientele produce some of the largest, most successful events throughout Colorado and the Rocky Mountain region. Lisa and Leslie, also known by many in the industry as "L&L," have established a reputation as a dazzling duo who feed off one another's strengths to craft celebrations unlike any other.

Affair with Flair specializes in creating unique social and lifecycle events for individuals, successful awareness and fundraising events for nonprofit organizations, and fun, meaningful milestone events for corporations. Their success has been a function of staying on top of and creating the latest trends in the event planning industry. Just as important as being on the leading edge of creative thinking, L&L partner with award-winning vendors in foodservice, venue management, entertainment, sound, lighting, and technology to ensure every event is the perfect production.

Events produced by Affair with Flair are recognized for exceptional creativity, tasteful execution, and for being managed in a way that meets the needs of every host. Every event must fit the personality of the host, and every event must captivate the imagination and engage every guest. L&L have made a name for themselves by adopting a "never do the same thing twice" philosophy.

Today's hot fashions are often an inspiration in event planning. We created a Juicy Couture-themed bat mitzvah party where fashion took center stage, complete with eclectic décor, eye-popping pinks, and a runway for everyone to enjoy being a true fashionista.

Above left: Two graduated floral rings of pavéd ivory and peach roses create a romantic dome for the bride and groom. Lined with sheer ivory fabric and adorned with curly willow branches holding fluttering petal strands, the circular huppah was constructed without a front or back, enabling guests to be seated on both sides, thereby creating an incredibly intimate atmosphere.

Above right: Creating custom, individual place settings makes guests feel welcome. Simple arrangements keep the table elegant and uncluttered. Personalized elements such as hemstitched napkins monogrammed with guests' names make a great statement and a memorable take-home favor.

Left: This wedding cake was set on a platform 20 feet above the floor, and was surrounded by an ornate golden frame to give the illusion of a portrait hanging on the wall. When the bride and groom cut the cake, it created the impression that they were in the portrait. We create one-of-a-kind presentations that guests will remember long after the event is over.

Facing page: When working in a beautiful setting, our goal is to integrate the existing décor into the overall look and feel of the party. The wonderful rose-themed art set on a rustic-style wall served as a dramatic backdrop, and the theme was finished off with brown lamour satin napkins folded into squares and sealed with miniature frames holding the couple's silhouette.

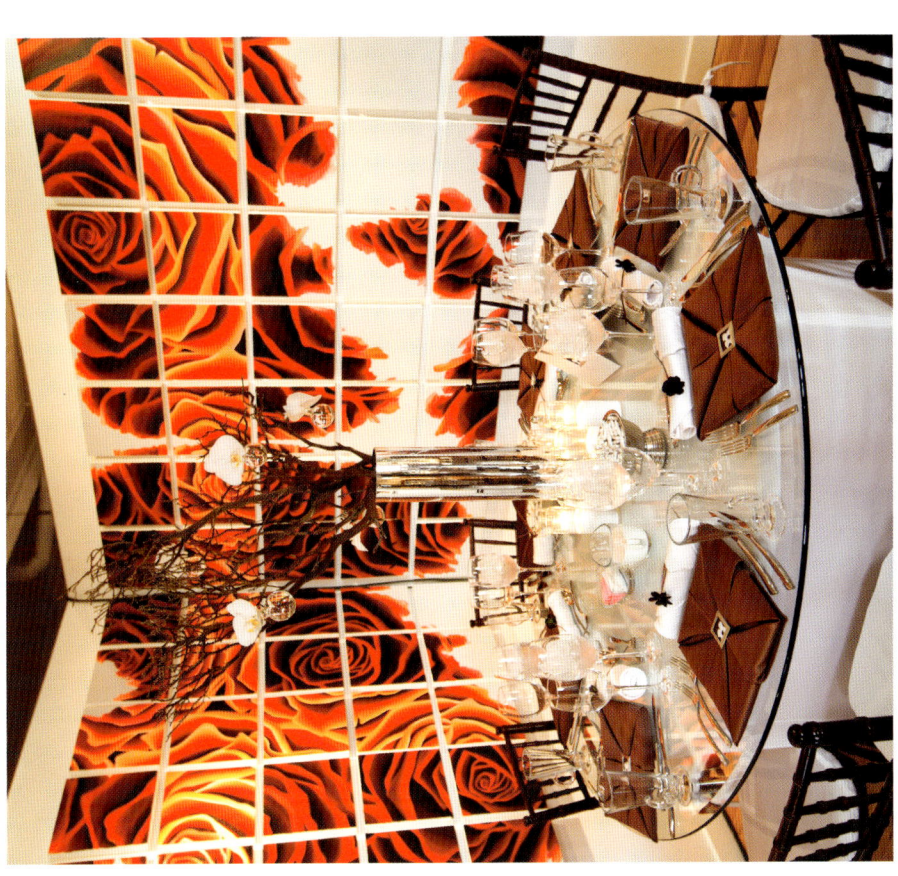

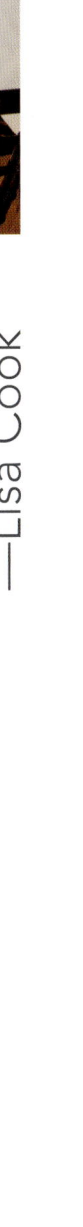

"The table setting can make all the difference in creating that special ambience every party deserves."

—Lisa Cook

Photograph by Eric Stephenson Photography

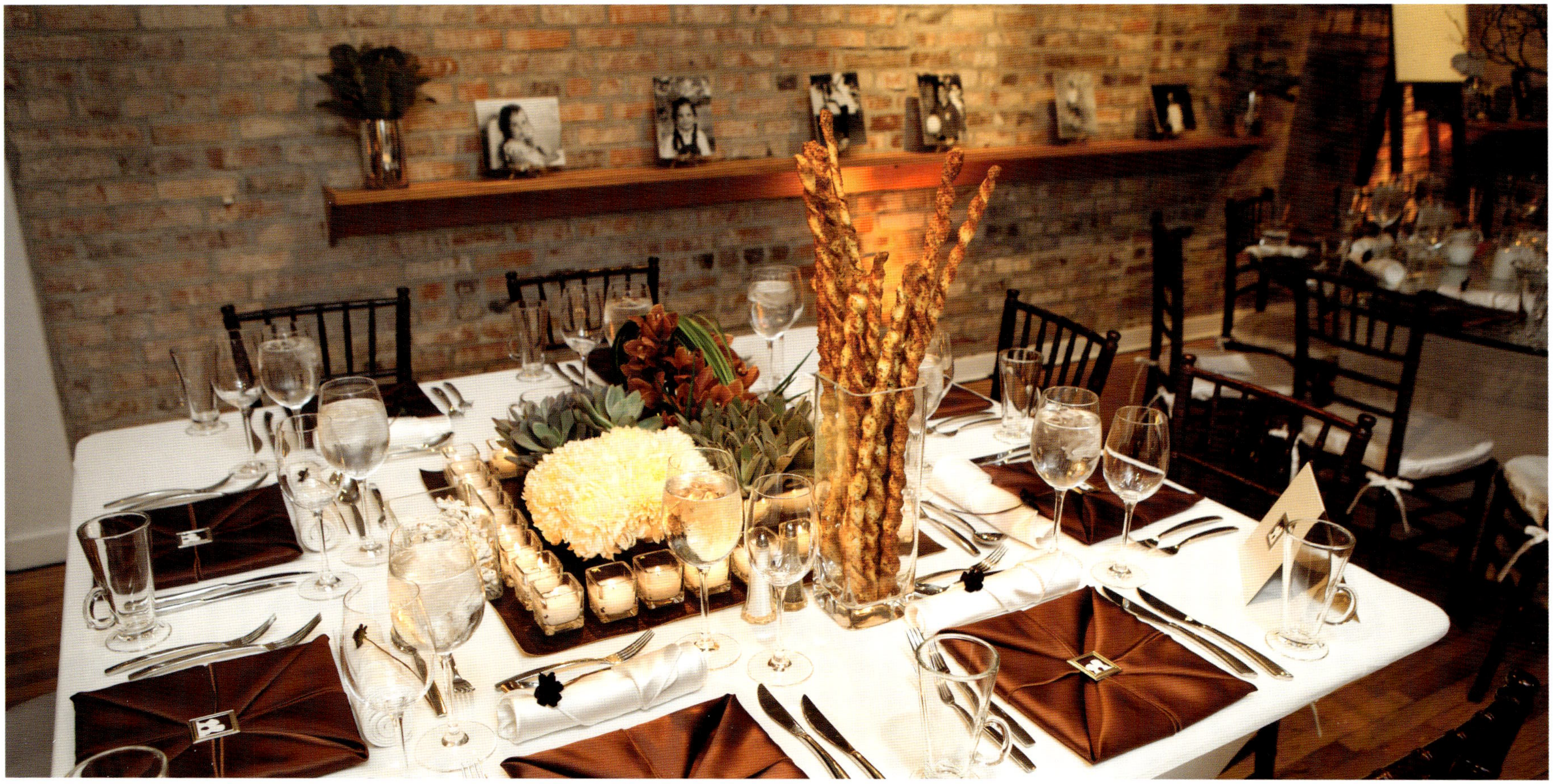

Photograph by Eric Stephenson Photography

"It's very important that the host and hostess feel like they are guests at their own event. We work very hard to remove the worry and to ensure our clientele is able to enjoy every single moment of their big day."
—Leslie Heins

Top left: The "salad quartette" made for an amazing presentation, as tasty as it was beautiful. The chef's creation included a white bean cassoulet in a silver eggshell on a gold ring, a baby spinach tower with teardrop red and yellow tomatoes, a chiffonade radicchio with lemon mustard vinaigrette, and a baby grilled artichoke stuffed with a truffle goat cheese mousse.

Bottom left and facing page: Celebrating the good things in life is why we do what we do. It is a joy to work with hosts to create themes and designs that bring the whole room to life. The ceiling of the ballroom was transformed using baffles of a beautiful domino fabric that created a stylish canopy, and the walls were wrapped in elegant antique gold shantung fabric and cummerbund.

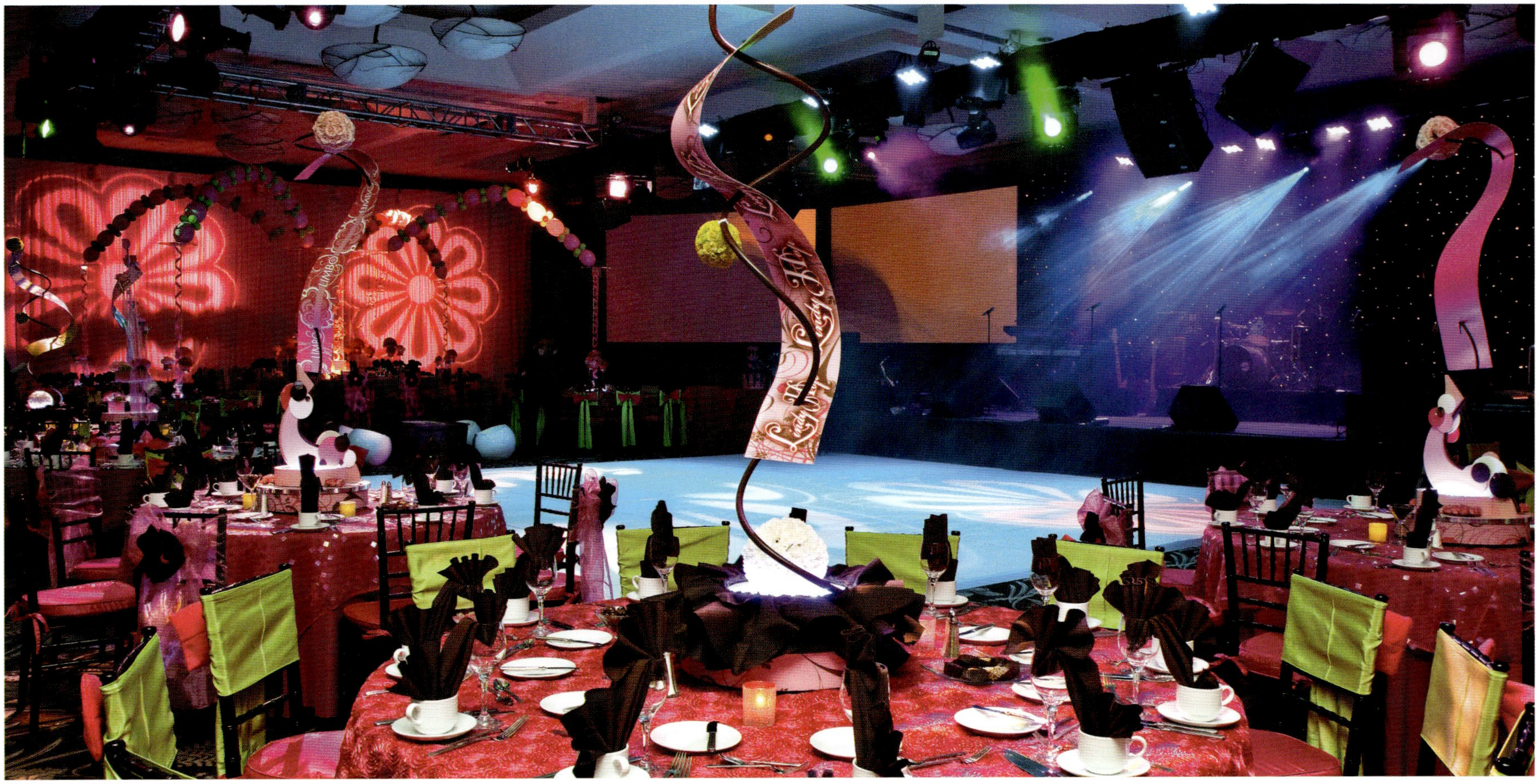

Photograph by Inner Image Photography

Photograph by Inner Image Photography

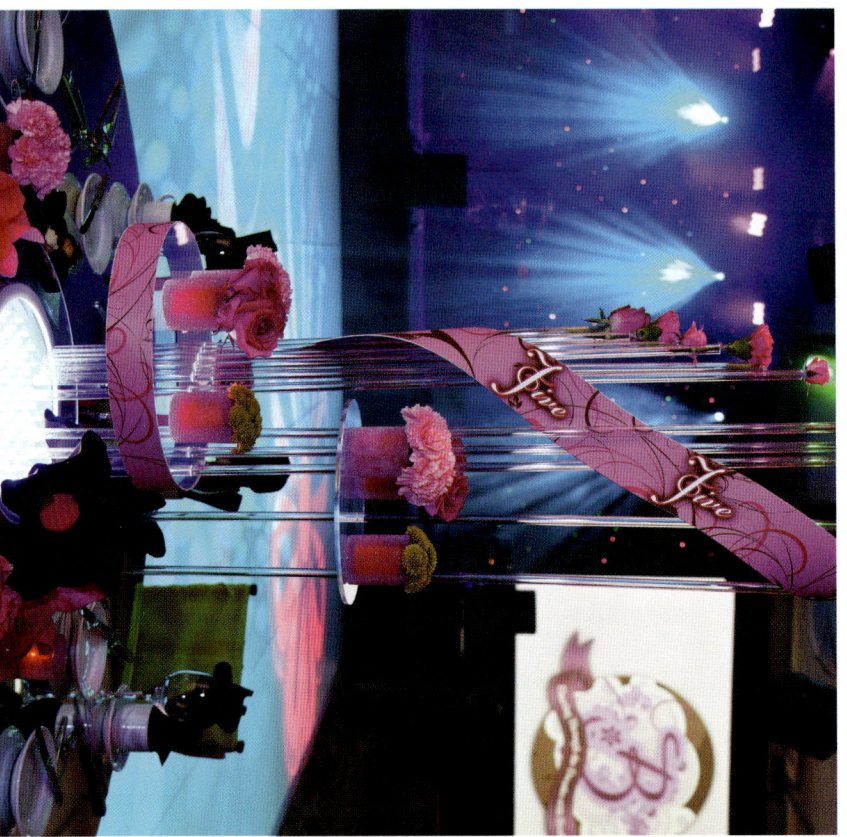

Above and left: Bright colors and intelligent lighting bring an electric vibe to a Dancing Through the Decades party. Large screens around the room displayed fun images, music videos, and digital messages sent to the guest of honor.

Facing page: The bride and groom's table stands out with two specially designed Queen Anne chairs for a platinum and rose-themed reception. Adorning the couple's table were antique silver candelabras containing pavéd roses and various cut-crystal hurricanes with floating candles. Mercury glass votives and cut-crystal bubble bowls finished off the table with a luminescent glow.

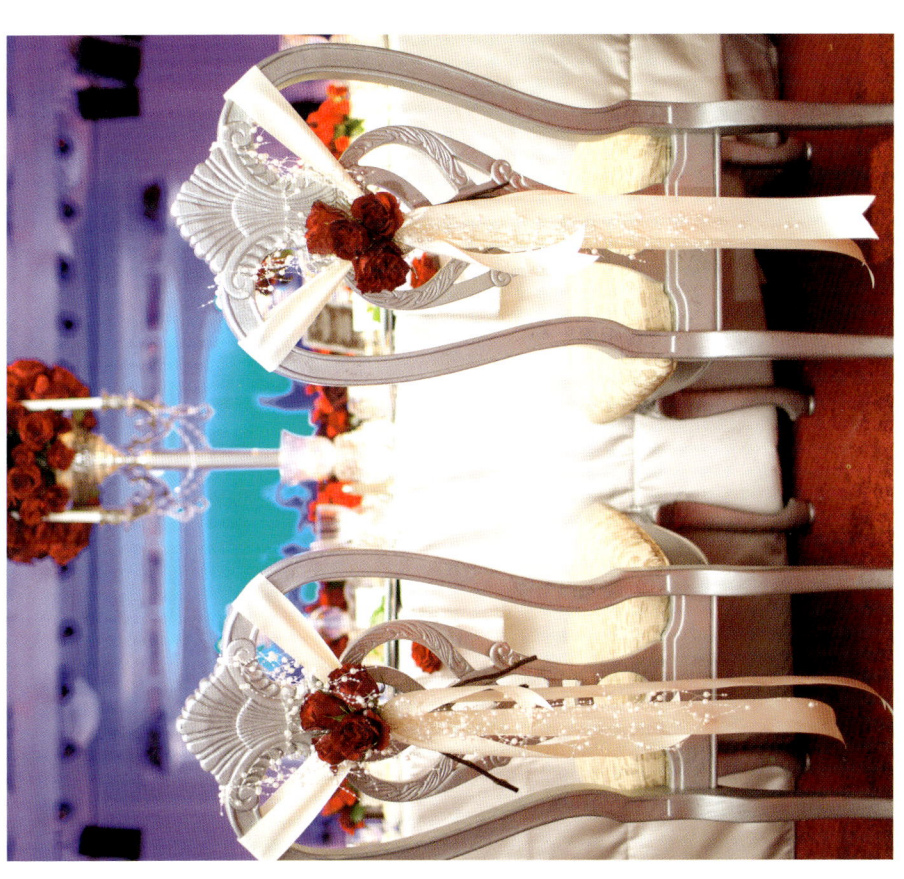

"People ask all the time about the most original event we've ever done and the answer is simple: whatever the last event we produced was!"

—Lisa Cook

Photograph by Julie Harris Photography

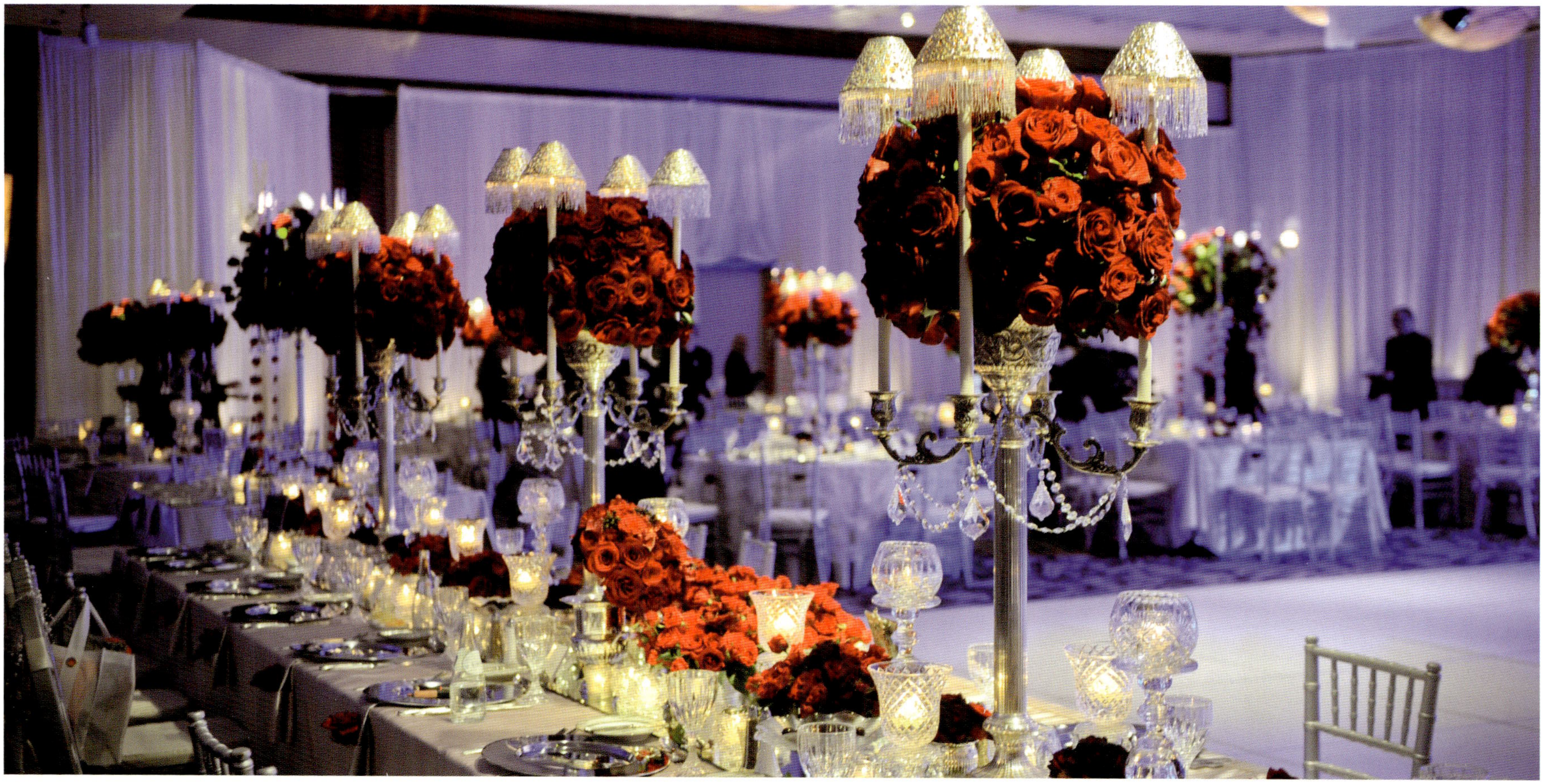

Photograph by Julie Harris Photography

Photograph by Eric Stephenson Photography

Photograph by Eric Stephenson Photography

"Each and every event should have a signature element that everyone will always remember."

—Leslie Heins

Right: The white cherry blossom tree, complete with hanging crystal strands, votives with butterflies, and orchids spiraling down the trunk, makes for a uniquely elegant centerpiece. We designed this effect so no view would be obstructed, whether a guest was looking across the room to the stage or across the table to another guest.

Facing page top: Using the grand splendor of Denver's Ellie Caulkins Opera House, we created a dramatic setting for two 15-by-20-foot screens that played a video montage capturing the beauty and depth of the soon to be newlyweds' very special relationship.

Facing page bottom: Individual cakes were placed on a rotating riser topped with a monogrammed vase and floral arrangement made completely from sugar. The display was one of a kind and complemented the romantic, fairytale ambience of the ceremony and reception.

When you hire an event producer to help plan an event, it's important to find someone who will push the limits of your imagination and exceed your expectations.

views

AMY TOLTZ-MILLER SPECIAL EVENTS

AMY TOLTZ-MILLER

For Amy Toltz-Miller, event planning means zeroing in on that special something that sets each host apart. Whether that means a passion for a particular sport, a dedication to a company's recognizable brand, or a penchant for decadent desserts, Amy will incorporate it into the event.

From coordinating bar and bat mitzvahs to corporate and high-end social events and even pro bono event work within the community, Amy delivers an affair that illustrates unique personality and flair. Most of the time, Amy is busy planning parties. When she isn't, she works within the Jewish community to make the world a better place.

Amy's vision and her close relationships with high-quality event vendors result in unforgettable soirées known for showcasing the host's personality. No theme is too extravagant for Amy, yet even the simplest wedding or charity event shines under her watchful eye. Her desire is to relieve her hosts' undue stress by handling all the details involved—some of which only an experienced event planner would look for. In her hands, party hosts, brides, and guests are able to sit back and rest assured that Amy has got it all covered.

It's the little details that guests remember long after they leave. A simply elegant huppah allows the couple to be the focal point. Cascading lilies mimic the love that rains down on the happy pair.

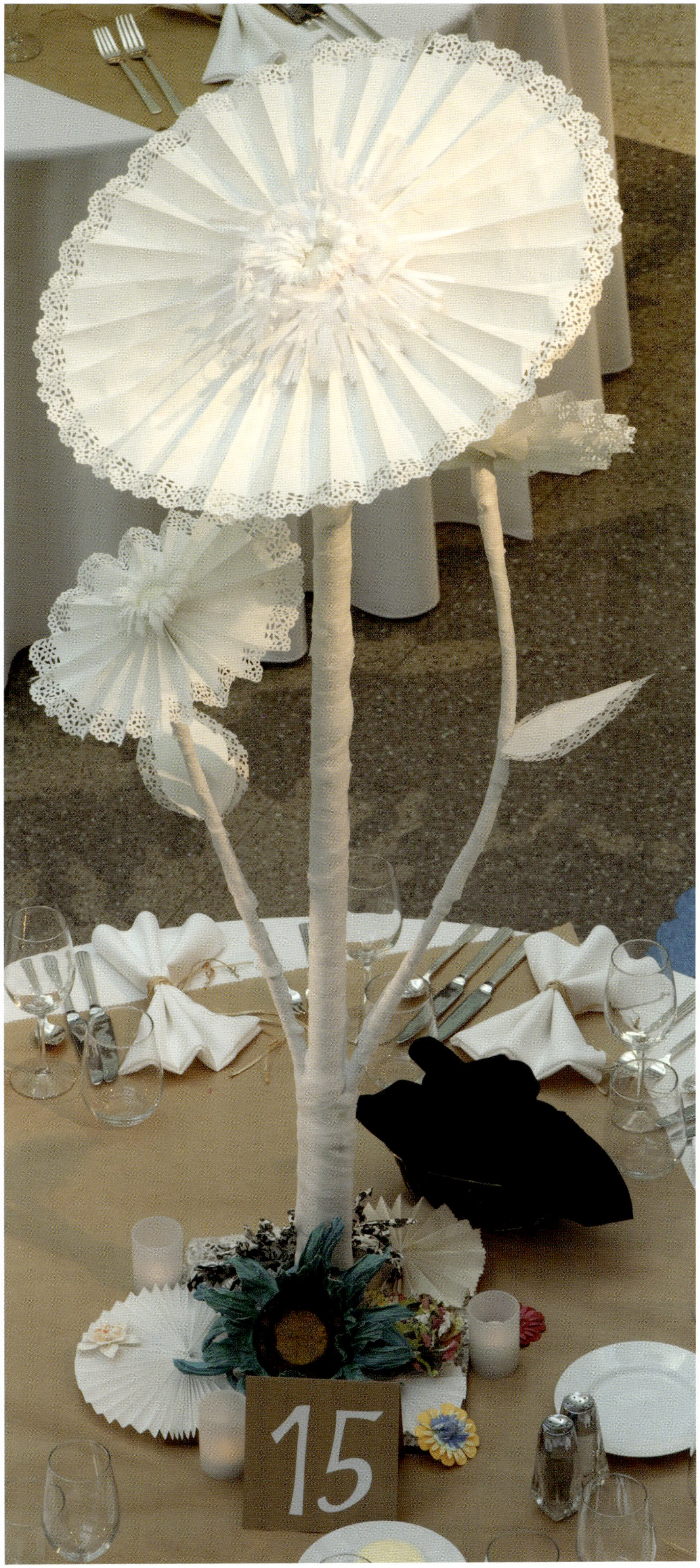

"Color, or the lack thereof, reinforces a theme."

—Amy Toltz-Miller

Photograph courtesy of Amy Toltz-Miller

Photograph courtesy of Amy Toltz-Miller

Photograph courtesy of Amy Toltz-Miller

Above and right: Dramatic décor transforms venues into the embodiment of the hosts' dreams. Bold colors are an impressive way to dress up a space. Draping luxurious, brightly-colored fabrics, choosing strategic lighting, and adding whimsical touches make an event anything but ordinary.

Facing page: Embracing whimsy in an event means that the décor will be memorable. Elegant paper centerpieces that resemble Victorian doilies and paper lilies on the huppah lend a formal tone to a more relaxed wedding.

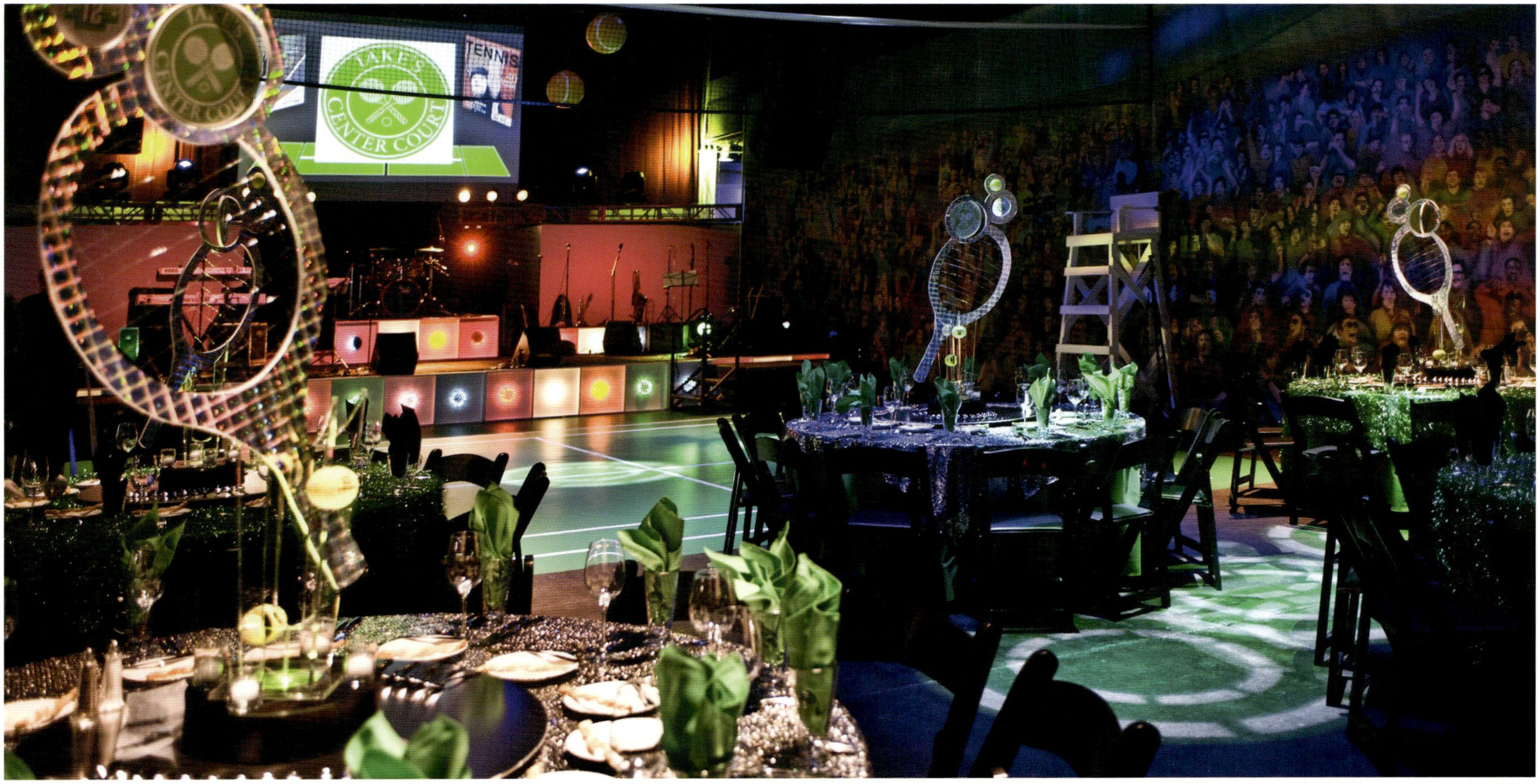

Custom elements make an event unique to the guests of honor. Embracing a tennis theme, we gave guests a dance floor in the form of a tennis court. Grass-green tablecloths kept the focus on the sport. Oversized tennis balls dangling from the ceiling and a net that stretches the length of the room are playful touches that aren't soon forgotten. A panoramic image of a cheering audience along the back wall made guests feel like they had stepped onto a court at Wimbledon. A live band and performers always make for great entertainment.

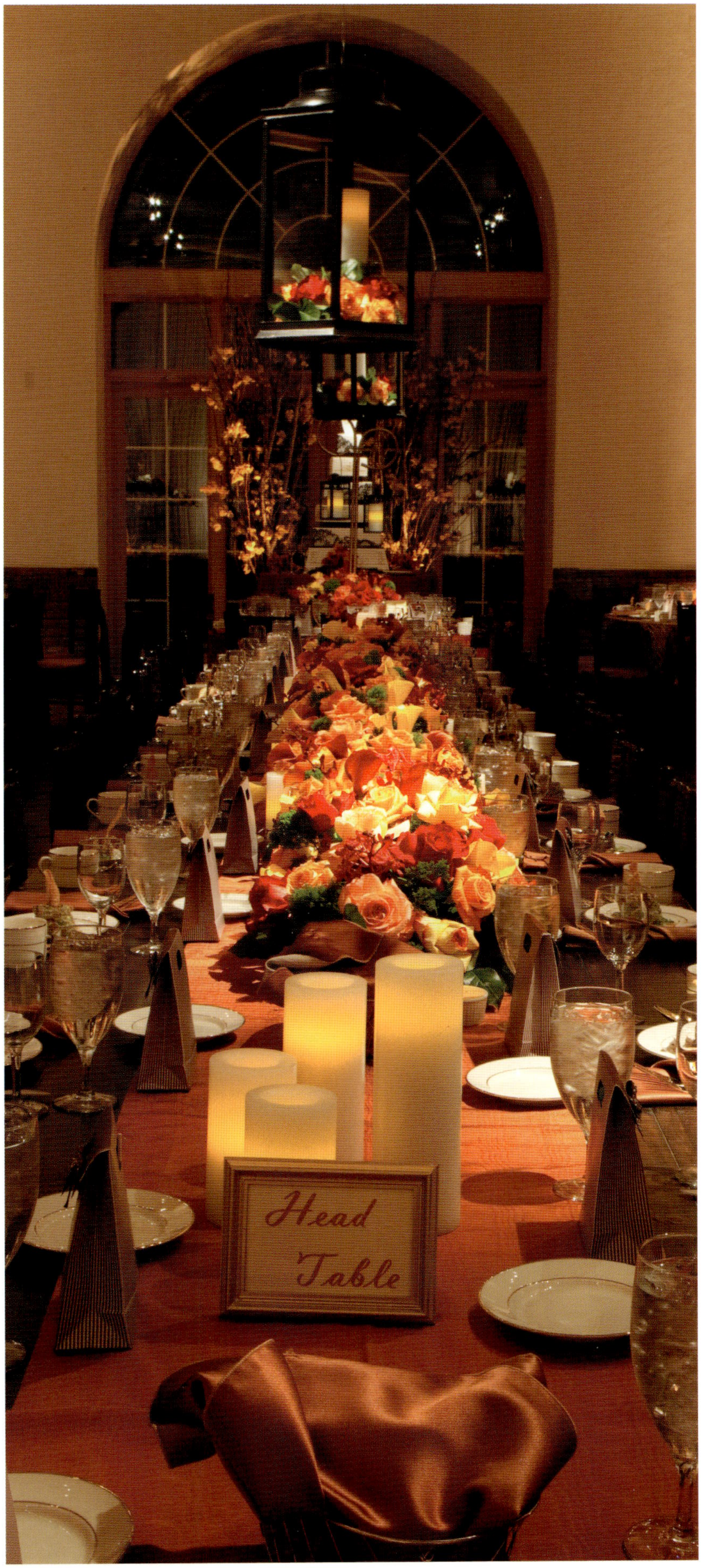

Photograph courtesy of Amy Toltz-Miller

Photograph courtesy of Amy Toltz-Miller

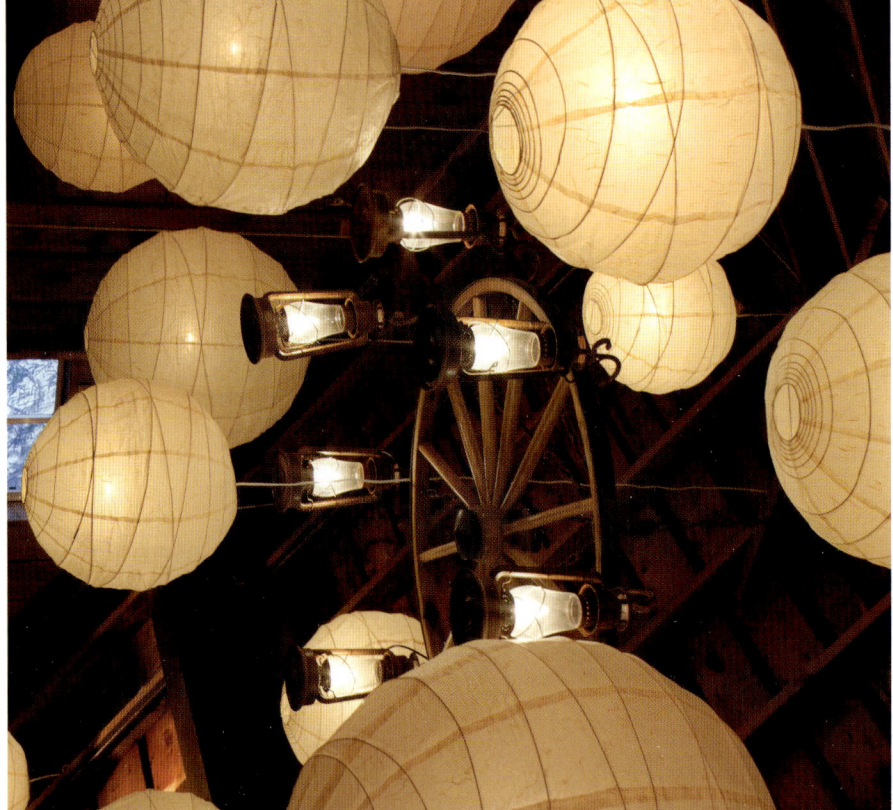

You don't have to go over the top with everything; sometimes the smallest details make the biggest impact. In a less formal setting, lights nestled among flowers and soft bows on the backs of cane chairs dress up the space without making it feel stuffy, and reinforce the natural theme. The proper use of light creates an intimate atmosphere, and special touches—like an utterly unique wedding cake—allow hosts to personalize the experience and really make it their own.

"Lighting makes all the difference."
—Amy Toltz-Miller

Photograph courtesy of Amy Toltz-Miller

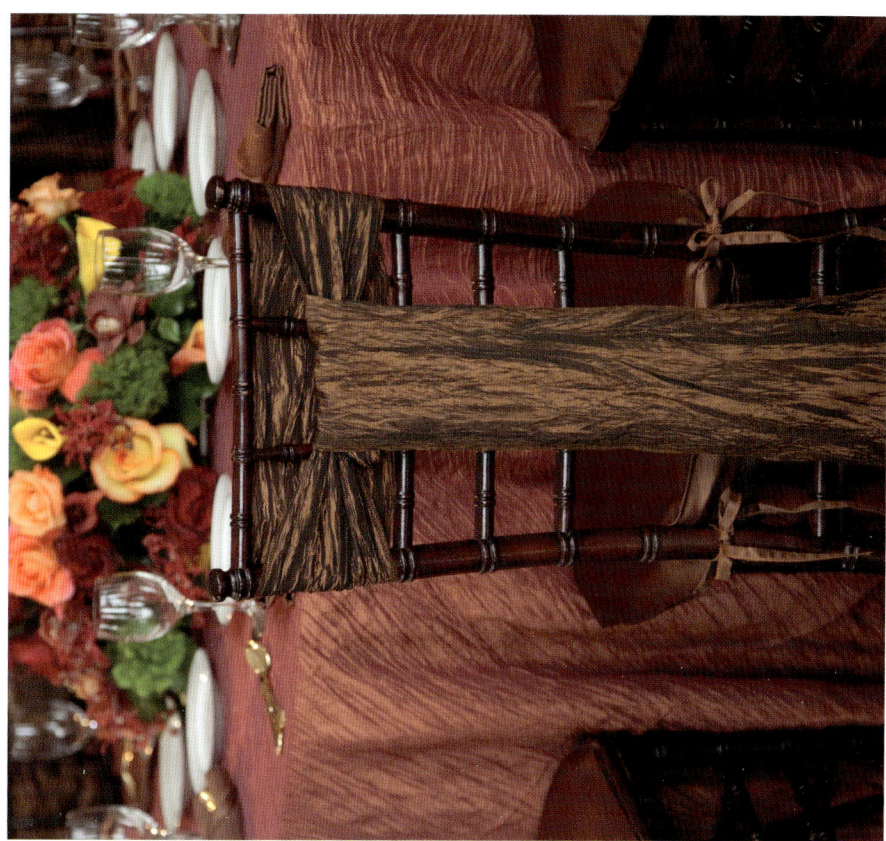

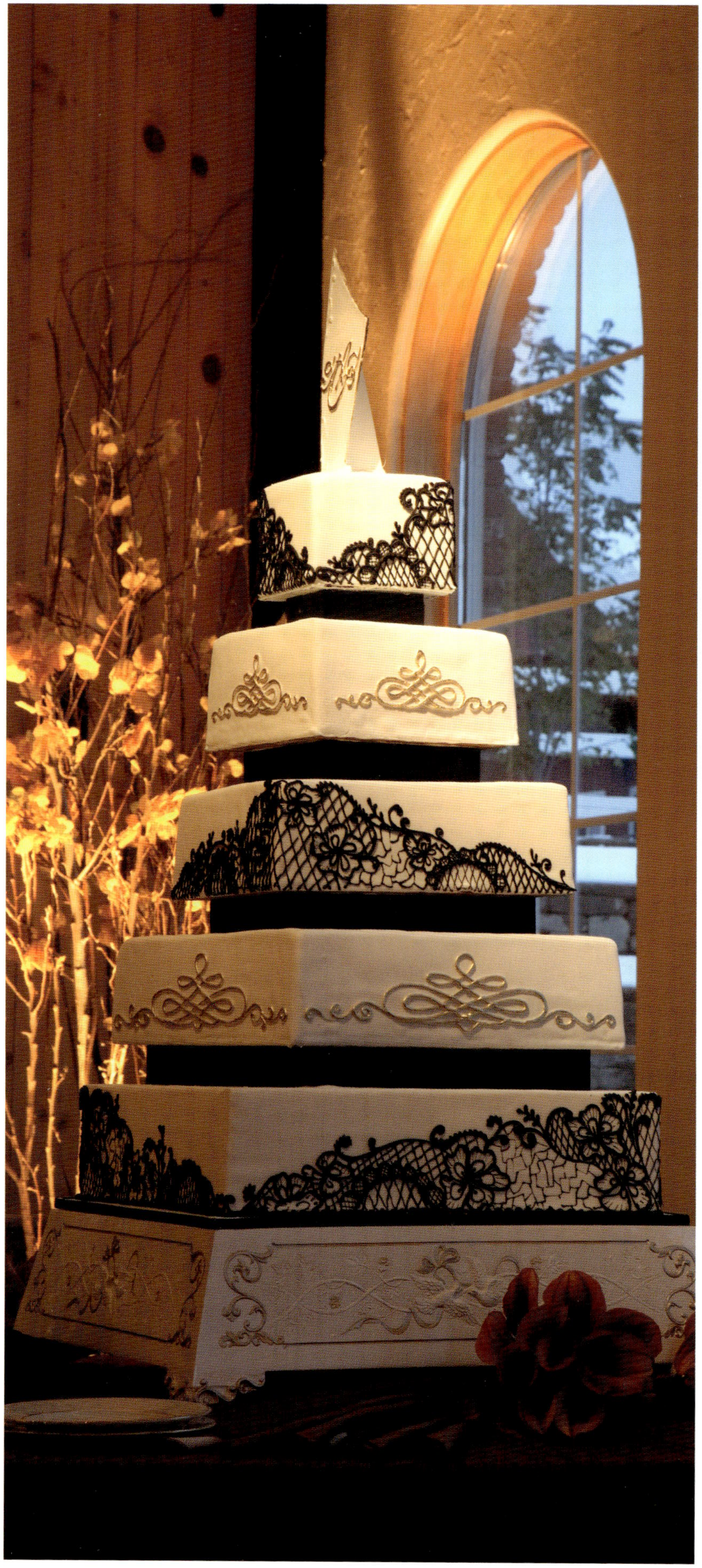

Photograph courtesy of Amy Toltz-Miller

"Never be afraid to play with scale; it adds unforgettable drama."
—Amy Toltz-Miller

A party should emulate the life event being celebrated. Circus performers, live musicians, and swirling centerpieces create an active party and a vibrant space perfect for celebration and conversations.

views

Find a planner who takes the stress out of your event. You shouldn't be running around worrying about individual vendors, wondering if the flowers will show up at the right time, or if the bakery got your order correct. The right event planner will take care of all these details for you so that you can focus on what's important: your guests.

CREATIVE EVENTS AND OCCASIONS

ALISA ZAPILER

A degree in design and more than a decade working as an interior designer have given event planner Alisa Zapiler the ability to view spaces from a unique perspective. Spatial layout, lighting, and the interplay of color all inform her vision, leading to an atmosphere which envelops its guests rather than functioning simply as a background. Besides a designer's eye, Alisa's skill set includes marketing, public relations, and business consulting. This experience may not initially seem relevant to event planning, but is extremely valuable for developing or adhering to an overall theme and working well with the myriad vendors it takes to shepherd an event from the idea stage to reality.

Since forming Creative Events and Occasions in 2003, Alisa—who embodies her company's initials as its "C.E.O."—has built a reputation as one of the most caring, attentive, and passionate event planners in Colorado. The creativity she contributes to events is matched only by the respect she shows each person who helps bring the social and corporate celebrations to life. Ideas, she often points out, are not something to be protected; in fact, they become more vibrant when shared with others.

Her work is mostly referral-based, with her clientele noting that she makes them feel like they're her only priority. While the actual event itself might seem like it goes by in the blink of an eye, the planning stage takes much longer. Alisa works hard to ensure that everything, from mapping out the big picture to selecting the smallest details, is an extraordinary experience.

A color palette of black, white, and sapphire formed a wedding reception held at the Denver Art Museum. The lighting design was a signature part of the décor. Shades of raspberry enveloped the room during each of the reception's big events: the introduction of the newlyweds, the first dance, cake cutting, and speeches. Candlelight was an important element to the couple. A profusion of votives lent a soft glow to each table. Acrylic boxes outfitted with neon lights underneath added an extra layer, an effect that intensified with each lighting transformation from pink to blue.

Event Planning | 47

"Pay special attention to the in-between moments."

—Alisa Zapiler

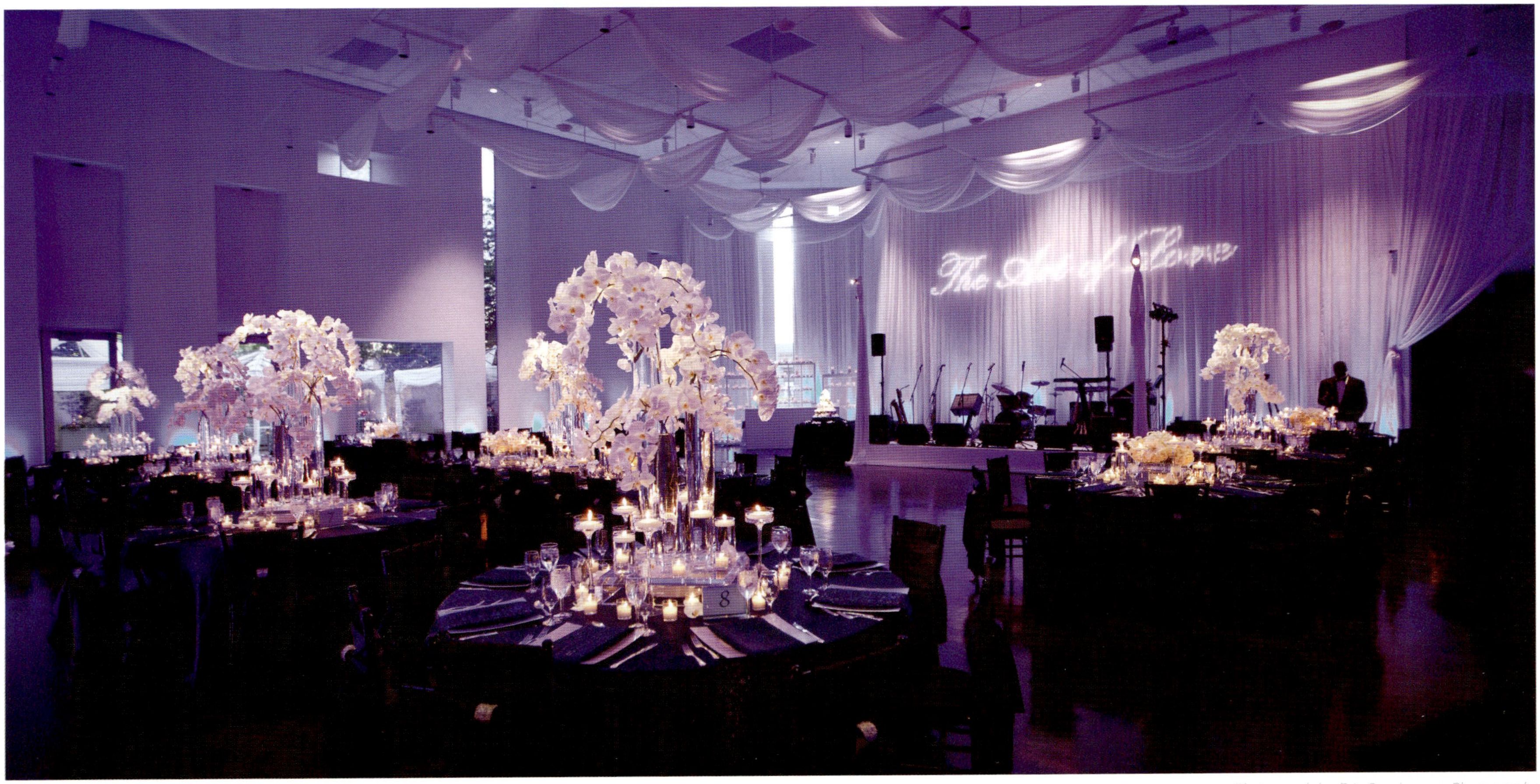

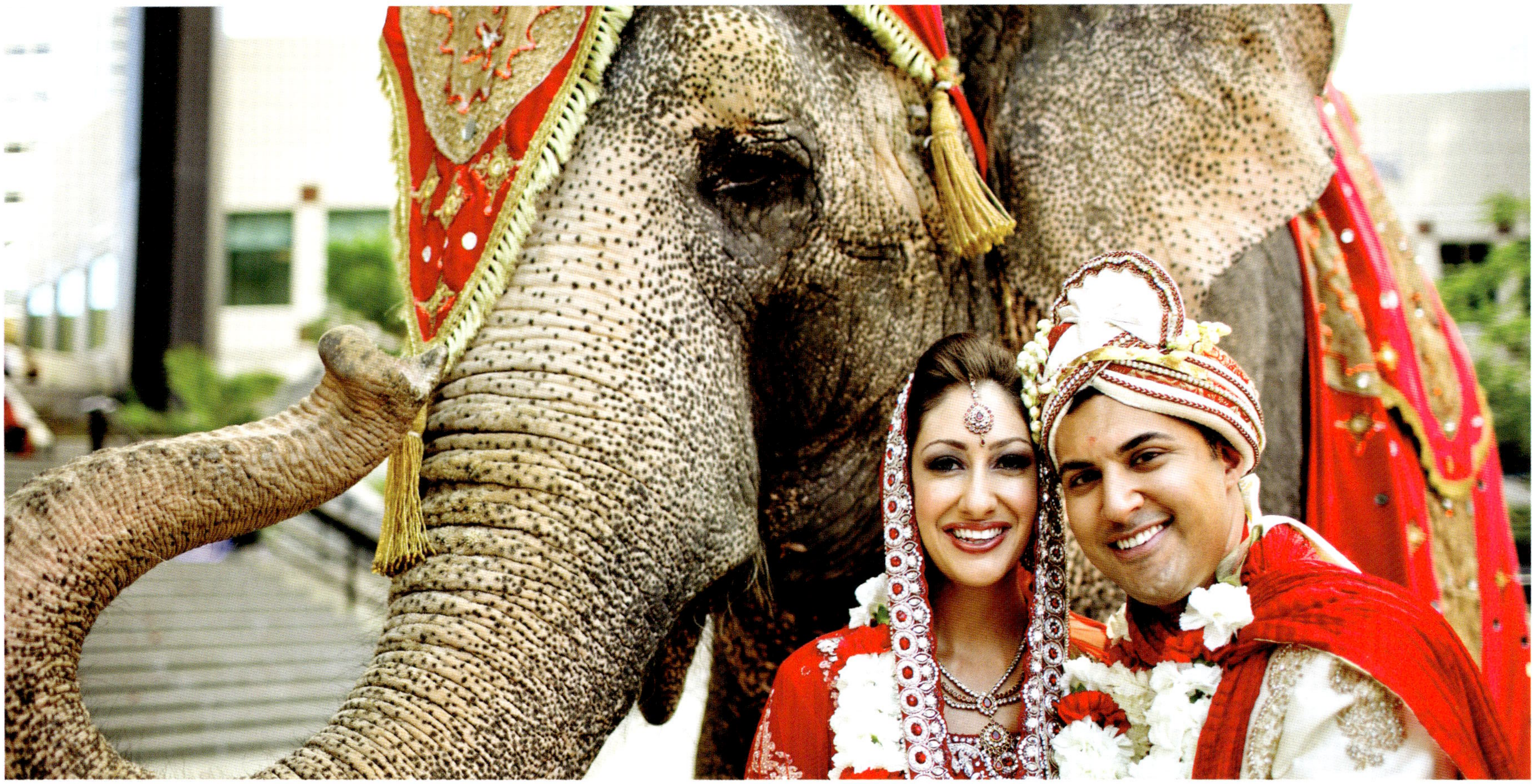

Photograph by Yamashiro Studio

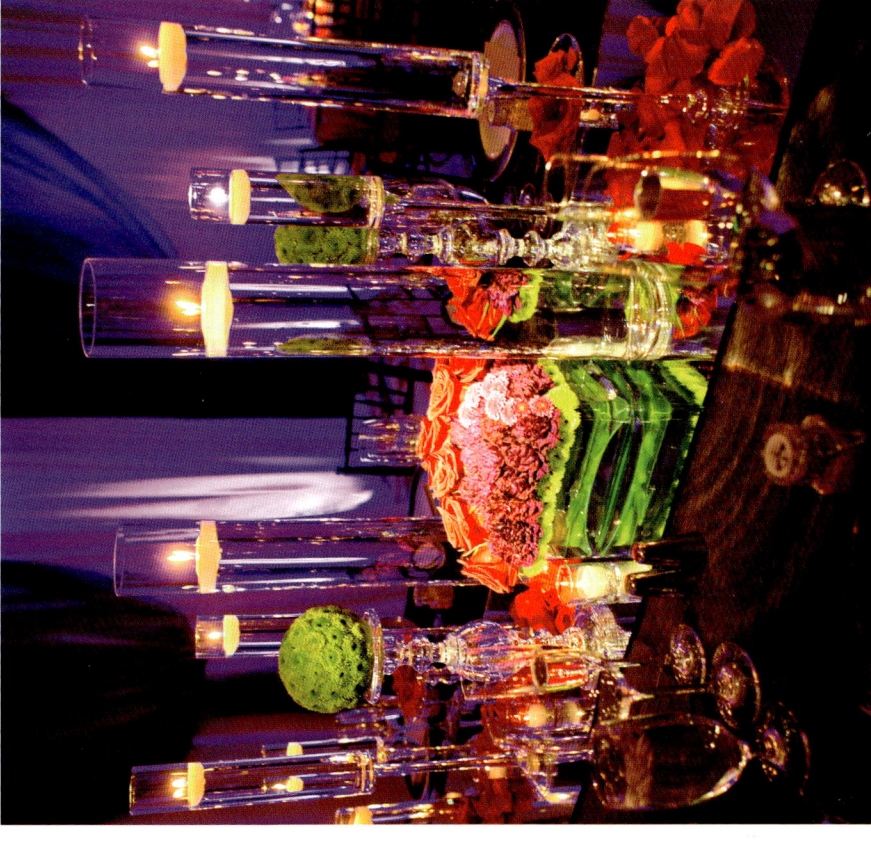

Above: A wedding that melded Hindu and Latin cultures together was an all day—and night—affair. Beginning with a traditional Catholic ceremony, the families then engaged in a multitude of time-honored Hindu rituals before taking to the streets for the *baraat*, a ceremonial procession of the groom atop either a horse or elephant. Our groom rode an elephant named Tai, who was brought in by her handlers from California especially for the occasion, thereby fulfilling the family's desire that this marriage have the auspicious fortune and good luck that elephants represent. As the groom looked down from Tai's towering frame, family and friends danced in celebration of the couple's union to the beat of drums. The joyful, colorful crowd surrounding the groom and elephant took 45 minutes to travel down four city blocks to greet the bride.

Right: The décor fused the cultures of the bride and groom, blending bold colors and rich materials. Each guest received a handmade blend of spices—also used in the reception meal—topped with the couple's personal logo: elephants trunks intertwined with a flamenco dancer.

Facing page: With "The Art of Love" as a theme, guests were encouraged to view the Denver Art Museum's exhibits before arriving at the top of Ponti Hall for a bird's-eye view of the fabulous setup below. After admiring the rare perspective, guests descended into the room and were greeted by an aisle of waiters bearing champagne. Every detail, from the orchids grown especially for the wedding to the rhinestone chair buckles to the softly draped walls and ceiling, reflected the time and thought the couple had put into their special day.

Photograph by Yamashiro Studio

Photograph by Eric Stephenson Photography

"Guests absorb a party at different levels. A well-designed party takes into consideration everything, from the overall picture to the smallest of details."

—Alisa Zapiler

Seeing your bride in a Vera Wang gown with a skeet-shooting rifle is a priceless indication that her elegant yet rustic wedding was a success. Held at Lazy J Ranch near Vail, the event was meant to combine delicate design with the bucolic beauty of a working ranch. Two tents, one for the reception and one for the ceremony and later lounge area, were draped in gauzy white fabric and hung with hundreds of illuminated paper lanterns. Hues of espresso brown and butter yellow laid the foundation for eclectic table décor, which included everything from birdcages to branches festooned with copper drops and flowers. The couple's custom logo, a lush bunch of wheat, was spotted on the aisle runner and appeared at each place setting as a few stalks tied with a leather lasso. A scotch bar, bonfire, and fireworks display made the day unforgettable.

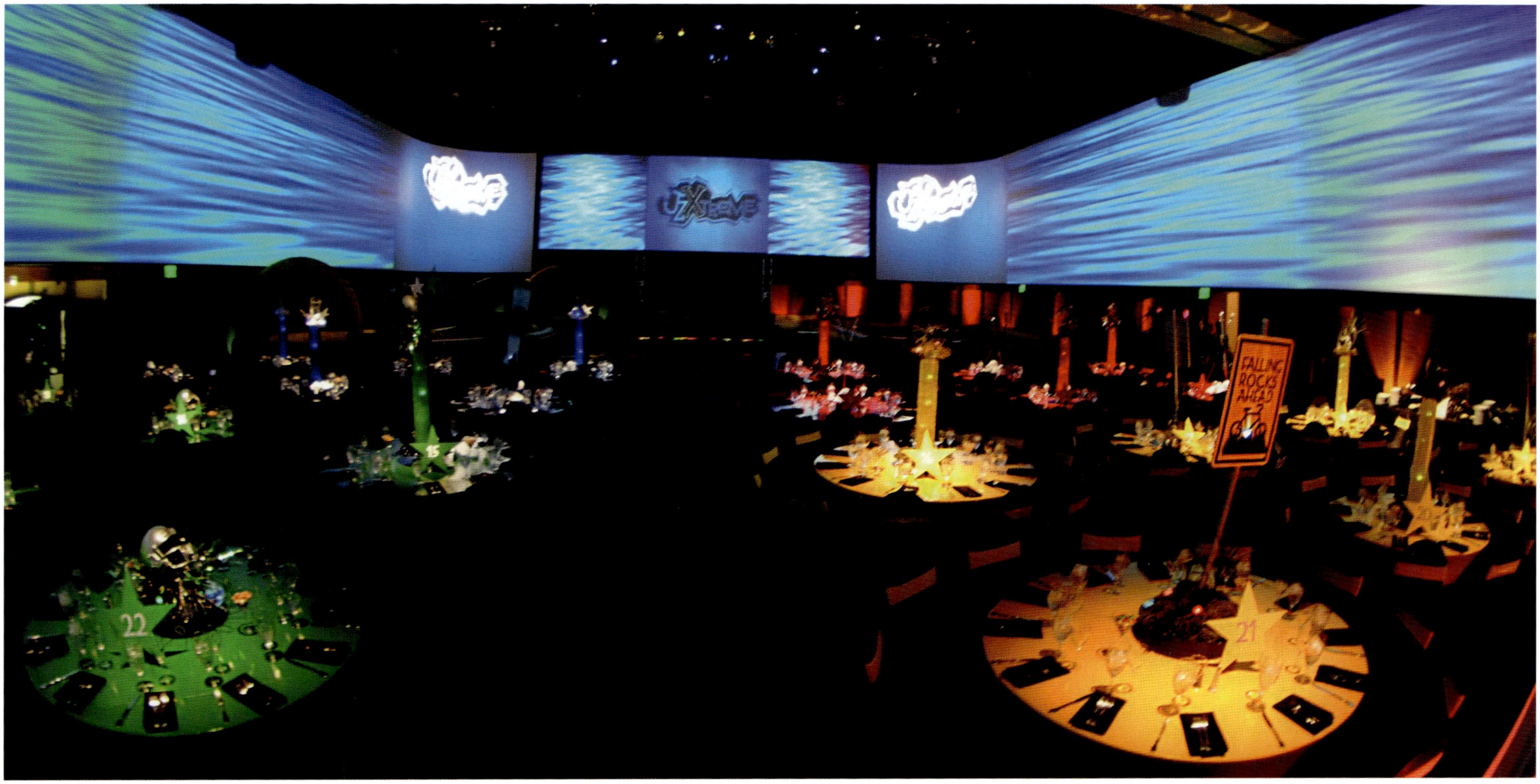

Photograph by WonderWorks Studios

Photograph by WonderWorks Studios

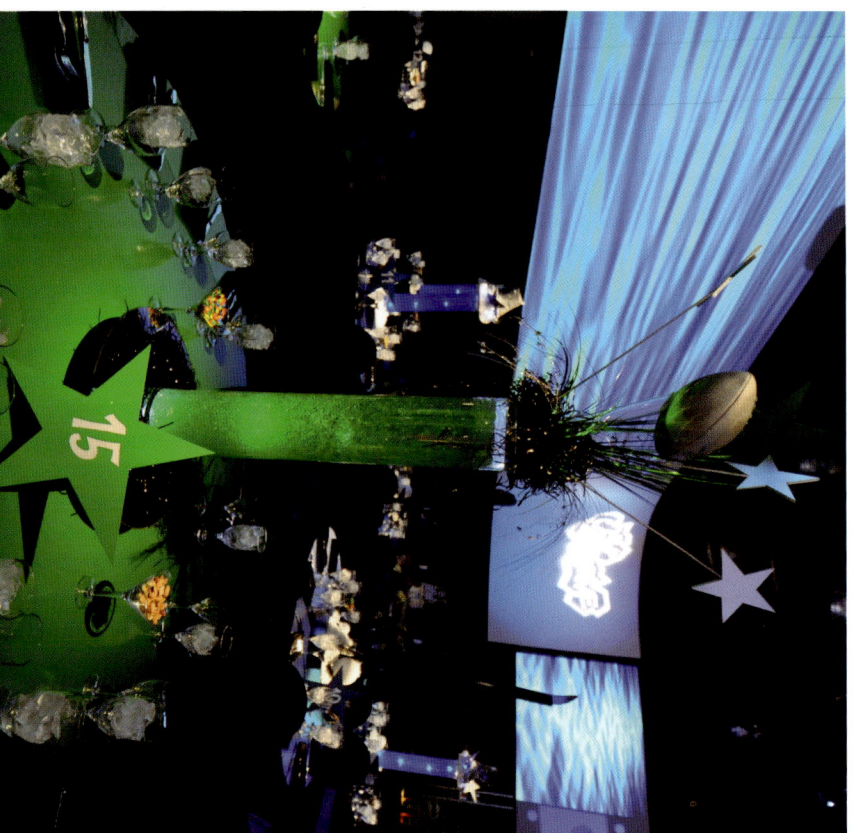

Above and left: Twin boys with a sports obsession celebrated their b'nai mitzvah with décor dedicated to skiing, snowboarding, football, and mountain biking. Unified color blocking divided the room into four quadrants—red, blue, green, and yellow—and each section was themed with its own sport. Patent leather table linens lent a high-gloss sheen while color bands on each chair accented the visual separation. Go-karts, gladiator wrestling, and other energetic activities were there to heighten the excitement of the day.

Facing page: At the same venue, an avid lacrosse player celebrated becoming a man by featuring his favorite sport at the event—the décor was comprised of real lacrosse equipment which was later donated to charity. Video screens, especially the all-encompassing ones at Infinity Park Event Center, offer a unique opportunity to surround guests with images and video. However, you have to be cognizant of the void they can leave if you don't consider the entire event. The lobby was themed to look like a real lacrosse field, with mannequin referees and stadium seats full of cheering silhouettes. Professional players from the Colorado Mammoth and Denver Outlaws were on-hand to sign autographs and pose for pictures.

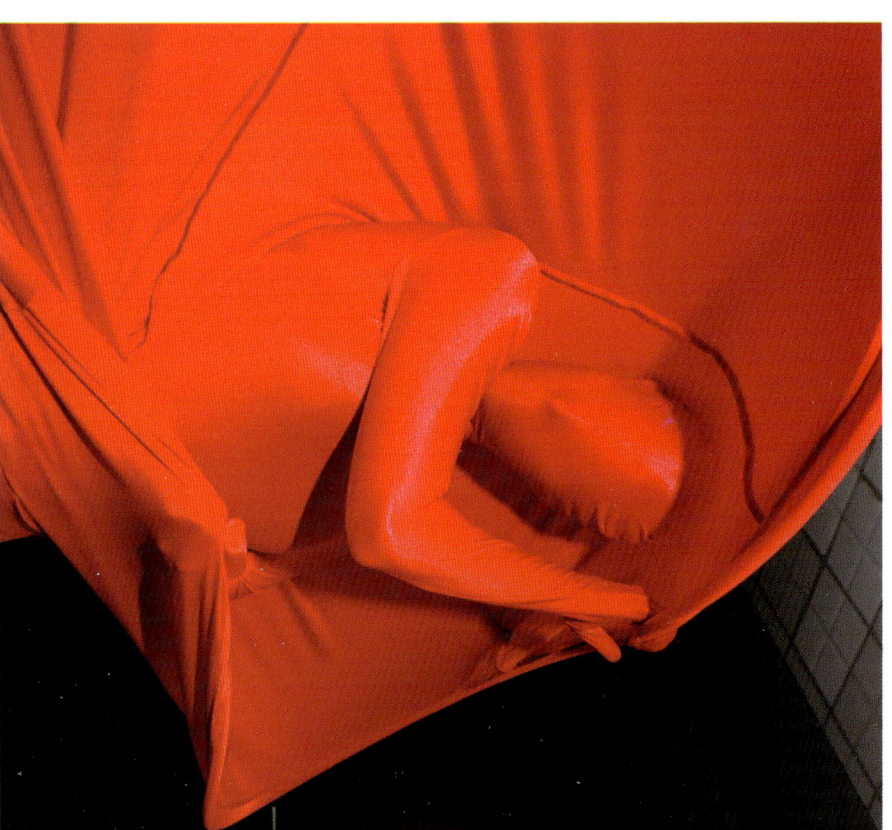

"An event's design and details should be palpable and unique."
—Alisa Zapiler

With his favorite childhood book *Red is Best* as inspiration, one boy used his bar mitzvah to help contribute to the (RED) charity campaign. This signature color also provided unlimited options for interpretation: a red carpet greeted guests, kids could get their hair sprayed crimson throughout the party, and a performer completely covered in scarlet Spandex entertained the crowd. Six sophisticated tabletop configurations, all designed with paved carnations and red as the connecting theme, provided texture to the room's décor. A full band kept adults happy, while human bowling and dozens of other activities provided the teens with high-energy ways to celebrate.

views

You're planning each aspect of your party separately, but upon arrival your guests are experiencing them all at once. Plan a grand first impression but don't forget about the other signature moments, like when they sit down to admire the table décor, taste the food, or head to the dance floor. When your guests leave for the night, what is the lasting impression? Anticipate every moment and how each flows into the next.

A Beautiful Memory

KATHY VAUGHAN

Imagine a lovely wedding where every aspect perfectly represented the couple, all the guests had a great time, and everything went smoothly. What's the secret behind success like that? It's Kathy Vaughan and her team at A Beautiful Memory.

Since 1995, Kathy has been utilizing her experience with nonprofits, formal training in etiquette, and detail-oriented personality to orchestrate exquisite weddings. More than just a profession, Kathy's work is really about the relationships she develops with engaged couples as she learns about their families, personalities, preferences, and dreams. In fact, when asked what events are on her top ten list, she says they all rank at number one because each family is special in its own way.

Kathy's versatility is a huge plus when it comes to making the big day meaningful. And her team and the professionals she partners with are a significant part of that talent. Kathy has practically done it all, from Indian weddings where she sourced all the materials and elements from India to an evening mountaintop reception complete with telescopes for star-gazing to a three-day event that included a petting zoo, wine tasting, fishing with fish fry, and onsite camping. No doubt unique in every way, Kathy's events do have two common threads: the guests' absolute enjoyment and the hosts' complete satisfaction.

For a bride who preferred chic modernity over extravagantly feminine design, I created a romantic environment that would stimulate guests. Lighting that changed colors throughout the evening and textures, like iron, wood, and soft fabrics, provided subtle interest and juxtaposition.

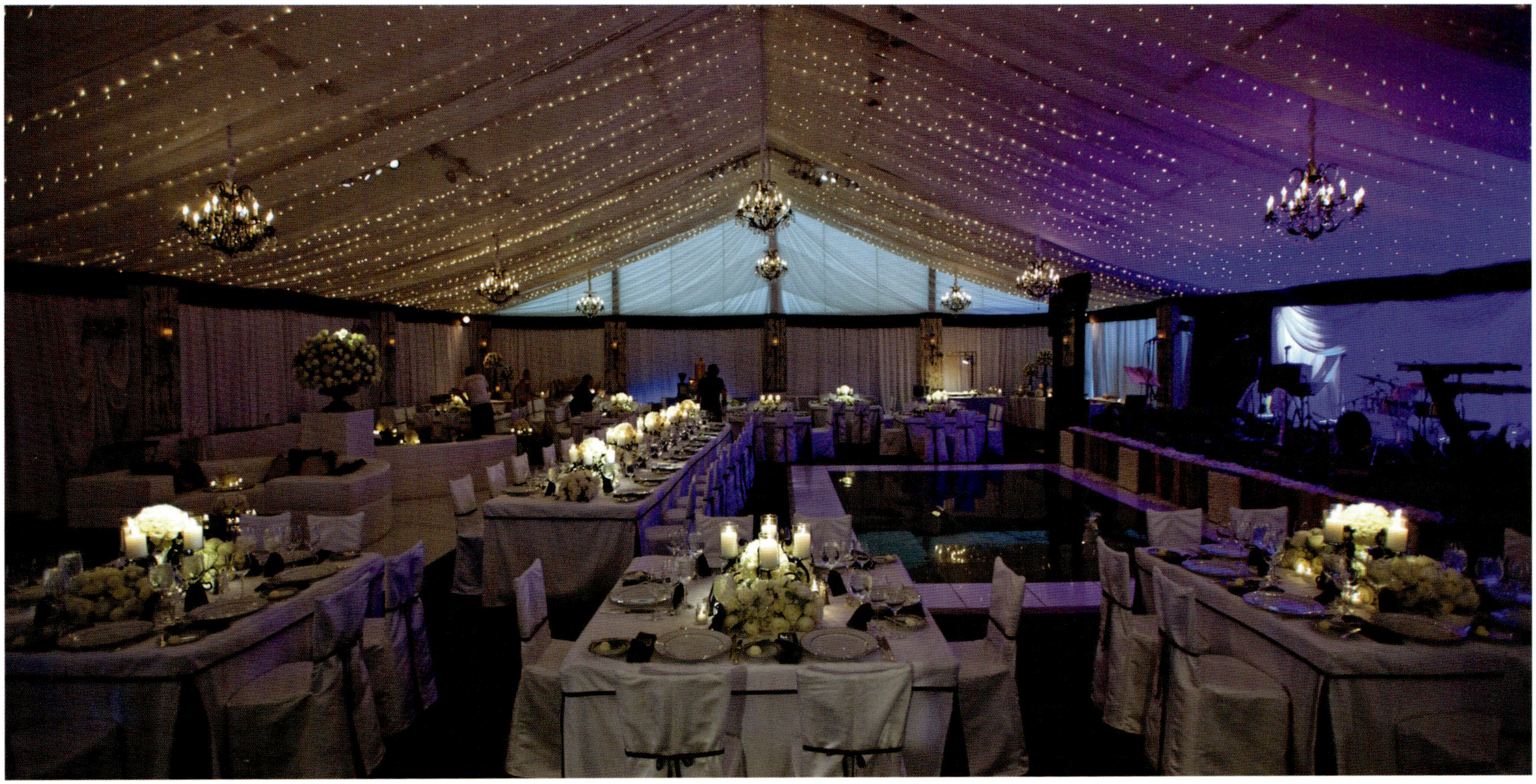

Photograph by broxtonArt

Photograph by broxtonArt

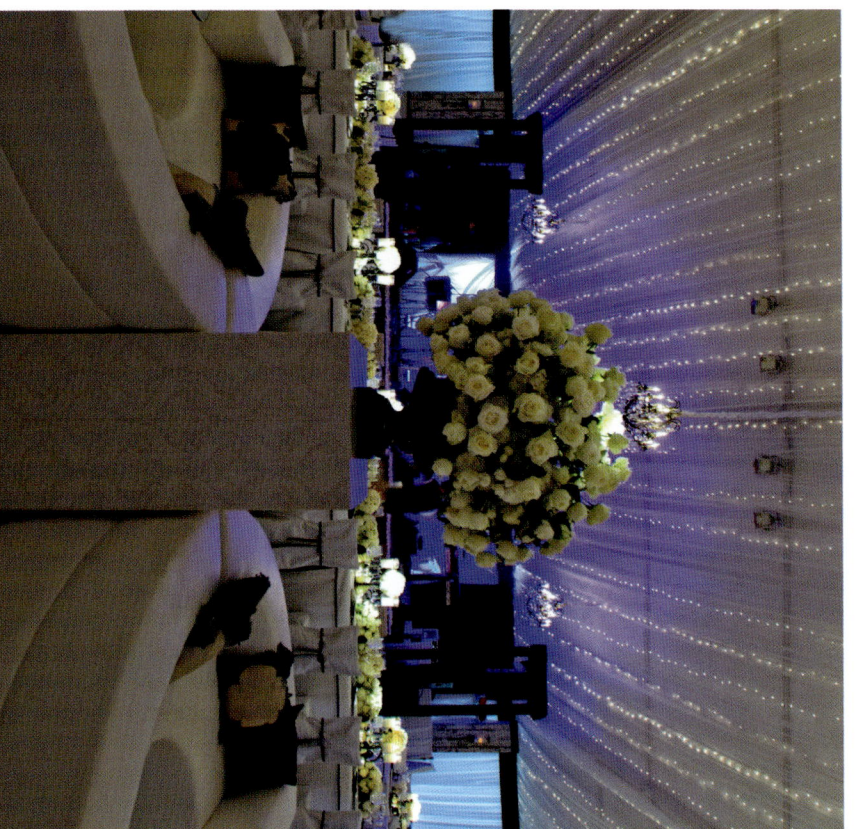

Above and left: In an exclusive neighborhood on private land, the tented event required all professionals to leave the land exactly as we found it—quite the challenge, which led to a two-week span from set up to tear down with 'round-the-clock security. Within the space, I created depth and a rustic yet elegant atmosphere that centered on lush flowers.

Facing page: To define a fall farm-to-table feel during the reception, I combined natural elements in autumnal hues, like mahogany tables and uncovered chair backs, with hints of formality, such as a ceiling canopy. The afterparty, held in the barn's hay loft, was transformed into a modern club, complete with zebra print chairs and lots of color.

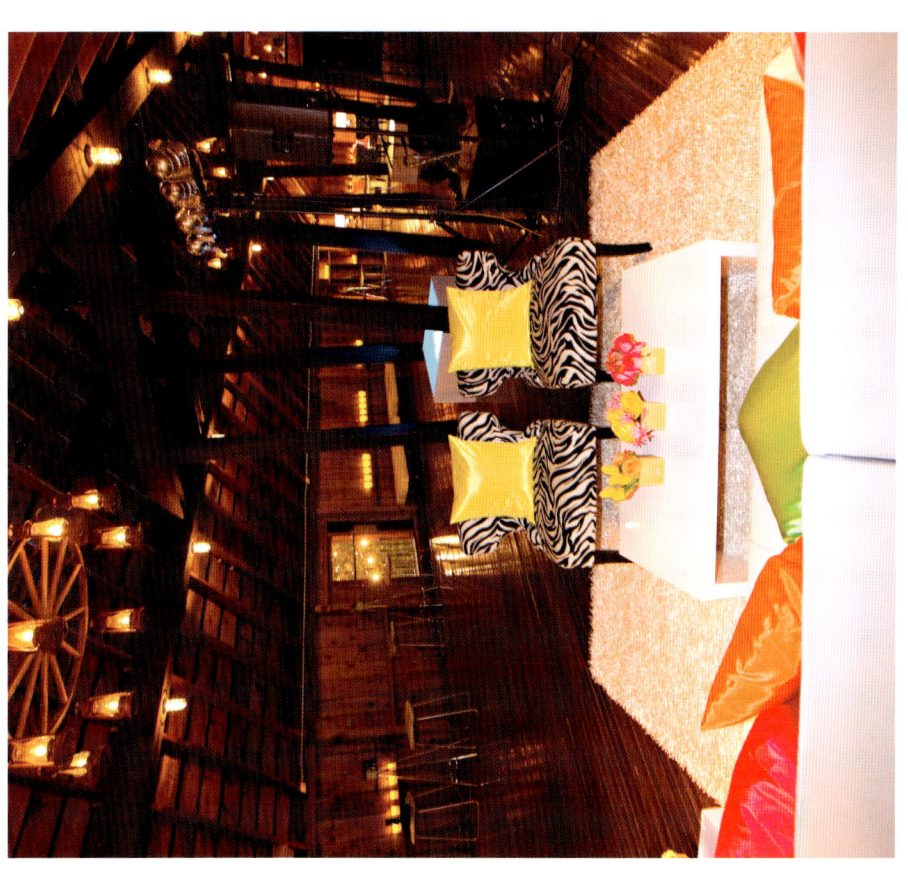

"Etiquette guidelines are just that: guidelines. But knowing what they are and the reasons behind them is important so you can determine which ones you want to follow or ignore."

—Kathy Vaughan

Photograph by Frances Photography

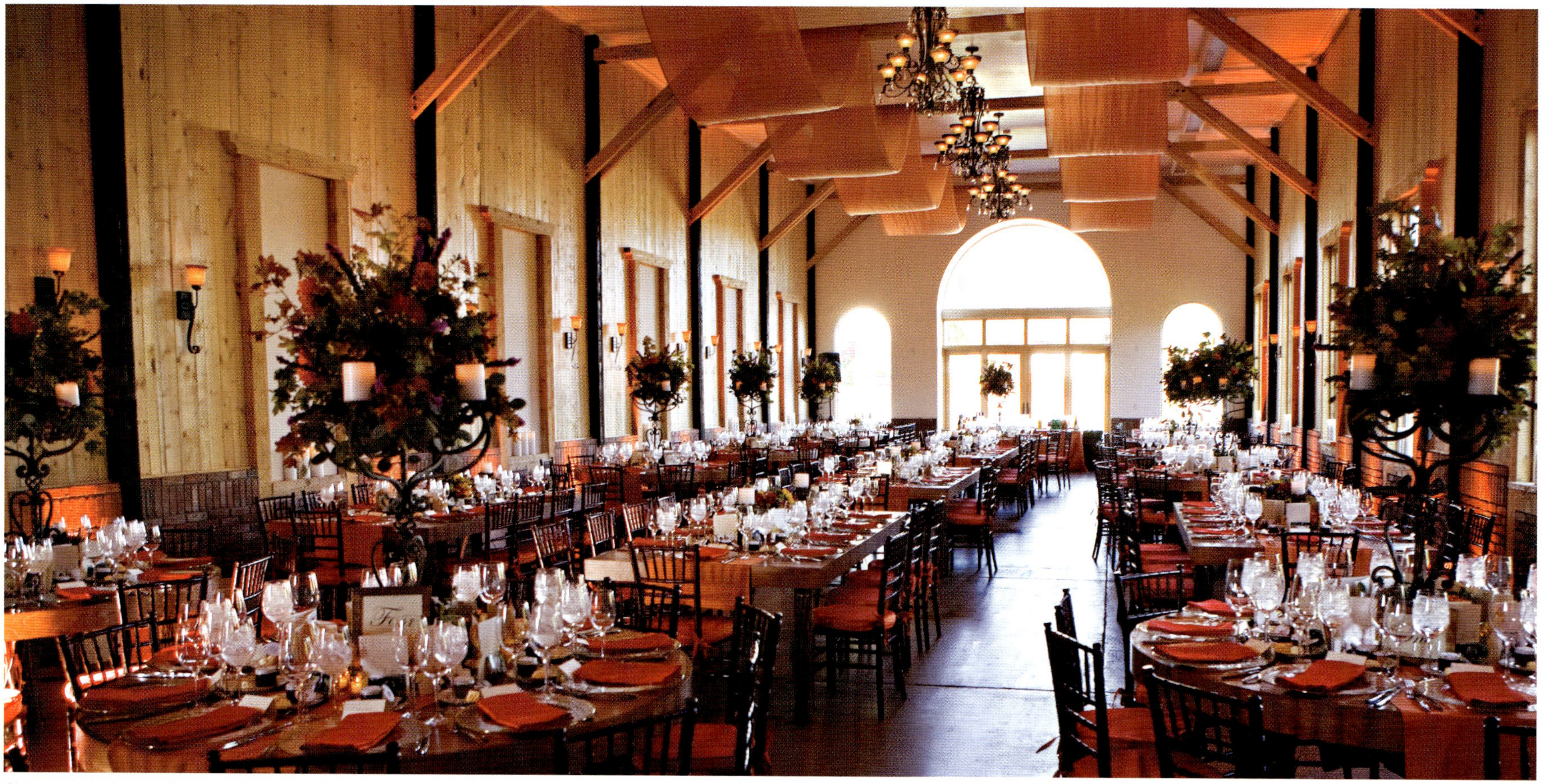

Photograph by Frances Photography

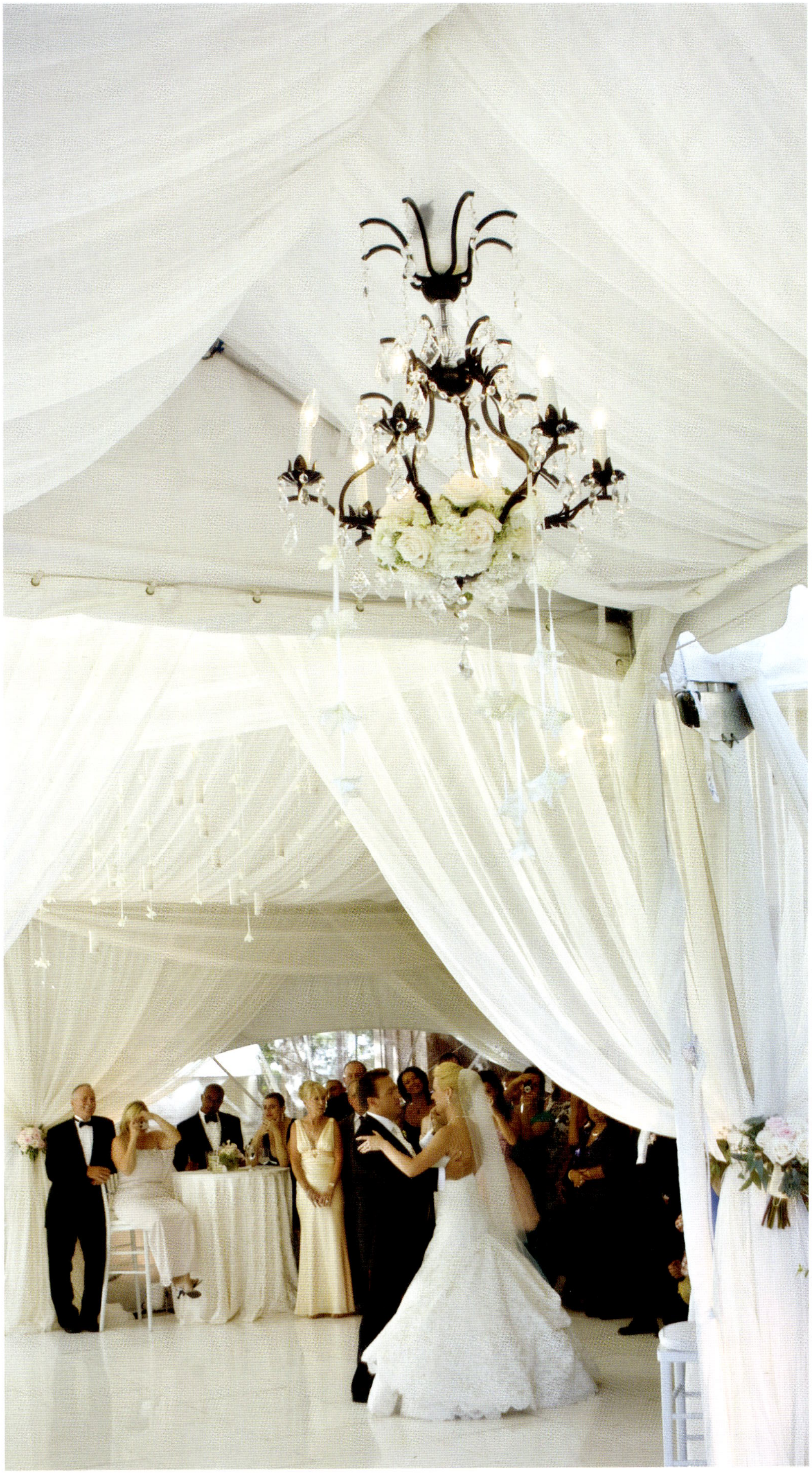

Photograph by Frances Photography

Photograph by Frances Photography

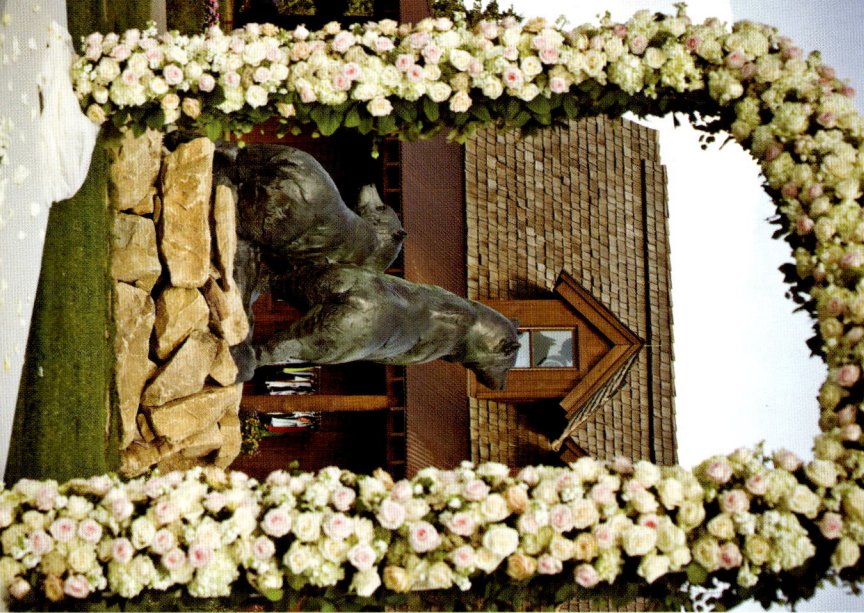

A private club in the mountains was the location of a destination wedding for a bride from the East Coast and a groom from Europe. The mature couple preferred a formal, romantic setting, and the bride's request for a little whimsy and magic prompted me to add in Cinderella-like accents, such as the flowers and candles hanging in the dancing tent. From the moment guests arrived, they were greeted with lush flowers around the outdoor ceremony arch that complemented the tone-on-tone elaborate details found throughout the interior spaces.

"Challenges bring a thrill to my work, whether it's coordinating security for celebrities like Tony Bennett or Kenny Loggins or shooing away porcupines who show up uninvited during an outdoor reception."

—Kathy Vaughan

A rustic arch and walkway of old barnwood planks built specifically for the event established a huge impression on arriving guests. Other details mirrored the modern take on Western flair, like the weathered barn door where table assignments were posted around a framed marriage "contract" that was written at their favorite watering hole when they got engaged.

"These are not my weddings; they are all about the bride and groom, their personalities, and what's meaningful to them."

—Kathy Vaughan

views

Having an event planner is helpful not only when it comes to organizing the pieces of the celebration, but also in coordinating with the family members involved. Everyone's family situation is unique, so it's nice to have one person whom everyone feels comfortable communicating with and who brings objectivity to the decision-making process. This ensures that the couple, family, and friends are able to enjoy the big day without worrying about anything.

CALLUNA EVENTS

HEATHER DWIGHT

Taking on the role of creative director, personal advocate, reassuring friend, resource maven, occasional family diplomat, and organizational expert is all in a day's work for the planning specialists of Calluna Events.

Calluna was founded in 2004, and has garnered recognition every year since as one of the best wedding and event planning teams in Colorado. From weddings and nonprofit events to intimate parties and large galas, the team at Calluna has done it all—and made each event unique with a keen sense of style and creative flair. After listening to the hosts describe their ideal event, the Calluna team taps into its years of experience and a network of carefully selected professionals to coordinate an event that embodies their personality and style throughout. In fact, the highest compliment the team can receive is when the hosts feel the event was fun, enjoyable, and, most importantly, an authentic reflection of their vision.

The planning specialists at Calluna are best known for their ability to stay calm under pressure, which is no small feat when you're orchestrating once-in-a-lifetime events requiring a multitude of people and facets to come together just right. Yet time and again they make that special day happen in such a way everyone involved enjoys the process and is overwhelmingly thrilled with the outcome.

Beano's Cabin in Beaver Creek was the perfect destination wedding locale for a groom who grew up skiing in Colorado and his bride. The venue, set in the middle of the ski area, is fairly remote so guests felt whisked away. The cabin's rustic but elegant ambience blended perfectly with their laid-back personalities. In cases like this when the couple is from out of town, our ability to be the eyes and ears on the ground in the planning stages is so crucial.

Event Planning | 65

"The uniqueness of each event makes me excited to go to work every day."

—Heather Dwight

Top right: Incorporating personal touches into every event makes it so much more meaningful to the families. The couple called each other "bread" and "butter," so they incorporated the nicknames into their wedding. In addition to incorporating the words on their chair backs, the reference was also brought to the cake with little bread and butter figures on top. We adored the favors incorporated into the table décor: vases that were all slightly different and included a custom placecard. This simple touch made guests feel welcome and was a more personal and unique take-away than a traditional favor.

Bottom right: The freshness of the ambience was a wonderful way to link the rustic feel to elegance. A few casual enhancements, like the bridesmaids' cowboy boots, also alluded to the couple's relaxed personalities and the location of the celebration.

Facing page: We are always excited to hear a member of the family or a close friend has the talent to help with an element for the event. For the Beaver Creek wedding, the bride's sister, Colleen Reid, designed and printed all of the stationery. The bride, her mother, and Colleen worked together to incorporate all the personal touches, which made everything much more special and memorable.

Above and left: At Devil's Thumb Ranch in Winter Park, one of our favorite Colorado venues, the surrounding 4,000 acres really allow guests to feel like they're in the middle of nowhere, creating a beautiful, intimate setting. The bride wanted to infuse the natural setting with an elegant fall look, which was achieved through color, texture of the linens, and candlelight for a romantic glow.

Facing page: Occasionally the weather just doesn't cooperate, so we always create backup plans A, B, and C with the couple and discuss them with all the vendors prior to the event. For a Boulder wedding, the plans paid off because we had to move the ceremony indoors at the last moment. We worked with the décor company to create the outdoor look inside so the bride could enjoy as much of her original design as possible. All the vendors worked together to transform the space into the reception within a very short timeframe.

Photograph by Jenna Walker Photographers

Photograph by Jenna Walker Photographers

Photograph by Recherché Photography

"I consider an event successful when everything ran smoothly and no one even knew we were there."

—Heather Dwight

Working with the décor team, we merged the bride's request for a plethora of pink tones with a few brown and cream hues to create richness in the St. Julien Hotel's ballroom. As with many of our couples who want to include local or sustainable elements, the bride and groom preferred seasonal flowers sourced close to home; peonies were a perfect solution. The delicious cake tied in many of the elements from the space but still maintained the simple, elegant feel the bride liked.

views

When trying to figure out what kind of event you really want, we suggest writing out a statement that reflects the style, vision, and priorities for the event. Then don't let yourself be swayed from the overall feeling you want to create. It's also helpful to envision what you would do if money were no object; then enlist the professionals to find creative ways to make it happen.

FAYE GARDENSWARTZ

Faye Gardenswartz has what she calls a "party eye." When asked to define what that means, she'll explain how she constantly sees possible party ideas in everything around her and is just waiting for the right person to come along and allow her to turn them into reality. To bring the astounding events she envisions to life, Faye calls upon her 30 years of event industry expertise and the strong vendor relationships she has carefully cultivated with mutual trust, respect, and communication.

Private, corporate, philanthropic—Faye is adept at managing all types of fêtes. She got her start in the event world as a volunteer heading up charity galas and then started her business by coordinating children's parties. Personal relationships developed, her clientele contacted her again and again as their lives evolved, and those same children she once watched blow out candles are now exchanging vows and celebrating milestones at soirées arranged by Faye. Corporations retain her services year after year, and her impressive list of past events is dotted with Presidents of the United States and countless celebrities. Still, Faye is selective enough about the events she coordinates so that each gets the time it deserves. That personal, one-on-one attention is what sets Faye apart, and it's not something she would ever compromise.

From supervising a thorough setup to solving sudden complications with unruffled grace, Faye is always on-hand to ensure that her events go off without a hitch, a trait that helped earn her the "person of the year" award in the Colorado event industry. And with hundreds of ideas still yet to come, there are plenty of opportunities for Faye to put her "party eye" to good use.

Turning a tent from ceremony site to reception space requires the utmost in organization. DesignWorks by Dave and Mike suspended the floral aisle treatment from the ceiling so that it could later become décor above the dance floor, hid dining tables behind temporary décor walls, and converted the ceremony stage to the band stage, all while guests enjoyed cocktails outside.

Art of Celebration | 74

Photograph by Lynda Hanshaw Photography

Photograph by Michael Roffino, DesignWorks

"Budget does not have to limit creativity."
—Faye Gardenswartz

Right: The huppah for my own daughter's wedding was inspired by *Fiori di Como*, the famous chandelier of flowers created for the Bellagio Hotel in Las Vegas by glass sculptor Dale Chihuly. I came to David Squires of DesignWorks by Dave and Mike with the idea and a book of Chihuly's work, and his company's creative and artistic talent took over from there. The Hyatt Regency Denver proved to be the perfect location to suspend the work of art, and with the assistance of the technical and lighting support of Fastlane Productions, the effect was magical. The entire team's commitment will forever be appreciated: a cluster of the actual flowers hangs from a tall window in my daughter's home as a reminder of that wonderful day!

Facing page top: For a 70th birthday luncheon, the family wanted the décor to reflect the guest of honor's beauty through the years. A profusion of flowers in coral, shell pink, lavender, and scarlet were offset by pearl topiaries on the elegant toile-covered table. A lovely, enlarged cameo of the birthday girl depicting her ageless beauty was the focal point of the room.

Facing page bottom: An elaborate luncheon to introduce friends to a family's new baby girl reflected the joy and playfulness of the occasion. Centerpieces made out of tall floral poles were connected table-to-table in a carousel fashion, creating a whimsical, totally pink environment.

Photograph by Michael Roffino, DesignWorks

"The hallmarks of a good coordinator are organization, creativity, and the ability to think on your feet."
—Faye Gardenswartz

Photograph by Jared Wilson Photography

Above left: Often a wedding will express only the bride's preferences, but it's surprisingly easy to incorporate the groom's style as well. While the ceremony was tinged with pink, feminine touches, the reception was entirely sleek, white, and sparkling thanks to Newberry Brothers and LMD Productions. The constantly shifting lighting design gave the room an exciting effect.

Above right: Tent décor is an important design element; lighting can work magic and the poles can be a beautiful addition to the event when covered with a spiraling rainbow of flowers or globes of brightly colored blossoms ascended to the ceiling.

Facing page: The wedding reception added a nightclub feel to the traditional setting by placing inviting couches and a four-sided bar around the dance floor. Even the dining tables were a mix of round, square, and glass tables lit from beneath.

Photograph by Stevie Crecelius

"The relationship between the coordinator and the party host is the basis for a successful event."
—Faye Gardenswartz

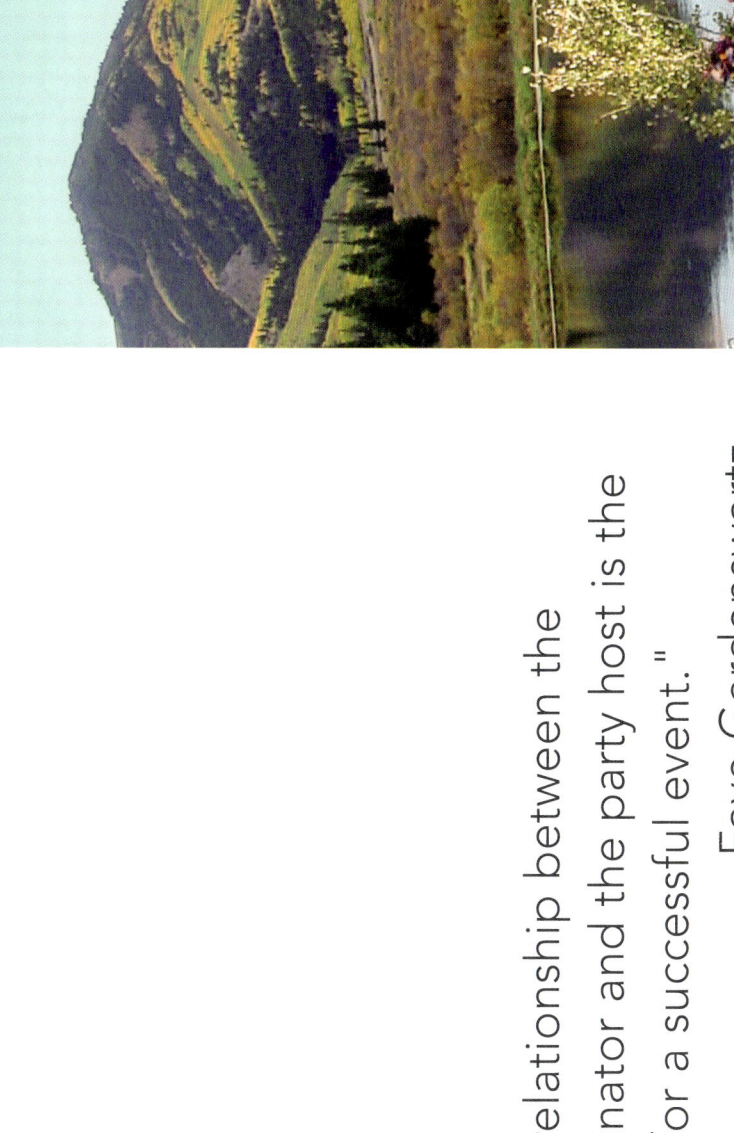

Right: Outdoor mountain events are very important and popular in Colorado, but they do take extra planning and precautions as weather here can change in an instant. After a picture-perfect ceremony in Aspen, the wedding dinner dance continued inside the lodge.

Facing page: A wedding held at the Seawell Grand Ballroom at The Denver Center for the Performing Arts had a definite theatrical flair. Guests were seated at their dining tables for the ceremony, and at its conclusion—on cue—a kabuki drop exposed the band playing and a beautiful floral wall created by Newberry Brothers. Simultaneously, the huppah rose up to the ceiling to become dance floor décor while other drapes pulled back to expose the cake and bars. Waiters traveled up the aisle with champagne, furthering the message that it was time to get the party started. That dramatic changeover was something the guests would be able to replay in their minds long after the evening ended.

views

Don't be afraid to express your dreams and pursue your vision. A good event coordinator should listen to your ideas and do everything within her power to make them into a reality.

Frosted Pink Weddings

KELLY KARLI

In similar fashion to the medical motto of "first, do no harm," wedding planner Kelly Karli believes her highest priority is to never take a bride's dream away. It is a special day for the bride, and she should be able to see her vision fulfilled.

Kelly, founder of Frosted Pink Weddings, can trace her compassion for others and desire to make dreams come true to her grandmother's legacy of making people smile, even while she was battling breast cancer. Her grandmother's influence was so valuable to her that Kelly named her company in her honor and makes a point of continuing her legacy of kindness.

A professional bridal consultant certified by the Association of Bridal Consultants, Kelly is one of the most highly respected wedding planners in Colorado. And her warm personality translates to an instant bond that develops into friendship as the planning process progresses. Growing up just minutes from Boston, where she was mesmerized by architecture, fashion, and design, Kelly has an innate eye for creativity and stays up to date with what's in style. Her metropolitan background exposed her to a variety of cultures, giving her the tools necessary to help create fabulous, stylish events of all kinds, from Indian to medieval gothic, contemporary to traditional. While she specializes in non-conventional and destination weddings, Kelly has a soft spot for planning weddings at home in the Rocky Mountains. Her dedication shows, so much so that her talents have been recognized locally and nationwide in such publications as *Style Me Pretty*, *Martha Stewart Weddings*, *Rocky Mountain Bride*, *Colorado View*, and *Colorado Brides*.

I blended the bride's love of all things pretty and floral with the groom's love of texture, line, and history. We transformed the room from light and airy to a medieval gothic lounge while retaining the elegance. The contrast, especially after such a traditional ceremony done in creams and ivory, was a fun surprise for the guests.

Photograph by Matt Alberts Photography

"Don't be afraid to push the envelope."

—Kelly Karli

Photograph by Matt Alberts Photography

The wedding was held at the historic Stanley Hotel in Estes Park, which inspired the Stephen King novel *The Shining*. We played up the connection by bringing in a Jack Nicholson impersonator and having fun with the history. In the planning stages, the bride and groom's idea boards were completely different, which enabled us to push some boundaries in combining hard and soft. The end result was very opulent, elaborate, and regal. Many of the design elements came from the groom's idea board, including the custom scrollwork at the base of the columns.

Photograph by Toni Axelrod Photography

"Have a Plan A, B, and C. If a wrench gets thrown into your best-laid plans, having options enables you to keep your cool."

—Kelly Karli

In Colorado, it's not uncommon to encounter brides with very chic style who want to get married in the mountains. The trick is finding a way to tie it all together in a modern mountain package. The bride loved the color orange, so we used vibrant splashes of it to add a juicy twist to her outdoor venue. With a guest list topping 200, the challenge was to figure out where to put everyone. We decided on both round tables and lounge areas. The white modern couches, white coffee tables with alligator coverings, and the white dance floor created an illusion of more space.

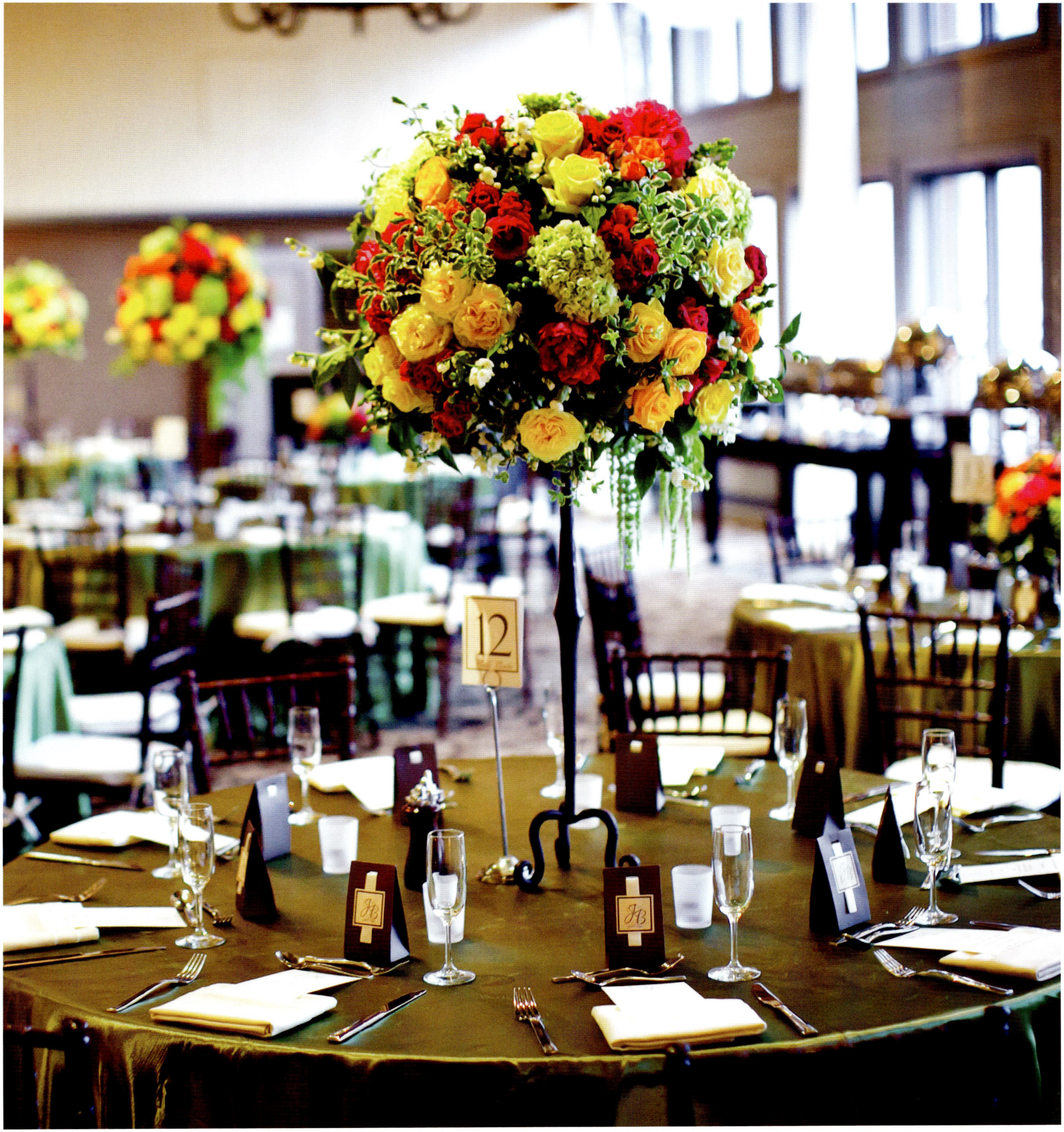

Photograph by Dreamtime Images

"It's the bride's job to take the groom's breath away, and it's the planner's job to take your breath away."

—Kelly Karli

The bride was definitely not afraid of color, but with such a vibrant palette she also didn't want to run the risk of the design looking, in her words, "too Bollywood." We went at the design very methodically, starting with one palette and then adding other colors. In the end, the balance between color vibrancy and visual grounding was pitch-perfect.

views

Your wedding day may not be perfect, but it will be spectacular. Slow down and take everything in. Your wedding day goes so fast and it's important to cherish every moment. And remember the end goal is you are marrying the love of your life. That is all that matters!

Special Events Design and Calligraphy

WALLI RICHARDSON

Event planners are influenced by the world around them—an exciting place where nature, cultures, and colors can provide inspiration—but it was from her grandmother, who was first a milliner and then an off-site caterer, that event planner Walli Richardson gained her first inspiration. With her grandmother's help, Walli learned early on how to view the world through artist's eyes. While she never got the chance to be an artist, Walli and some of her friends started planning over-the-top parties before such extravagant events were the norm. The bigger and crazier, the better, and she found that planning parties satisfied her creative desires.

Yet it was a move from California to Colorado that provided Walli with the opportunity to seize her dream. Rather than continuing her career in education, she turned instead to event planning and began learning as much as possible from industry experts. Utilizing her education in calligraphy, she began making contacts within the Denver community, starting by working with stationery companies in the area. Like her grandmother before her, she worked for an off-site caterer, as well as an event design firm. The towering heights she has scaled as founder of Special Events Design and Calligraphy don't faze Walli; if anything, they prepared her to meet the great heights of her hosts' imaginations. While she is diligent in making sure her hosts' dreams are actualized, she doesn't take herself too seriously, opting instead to remain flexible and fun.

Coming up with designs that honor the host can be challenging but ultimately very rewarding. Knowing where to draw the line between elegance and going over the top is the key to pulling off an event that guests will remember for its beauty. Balancing cascading crystals against a monochromatic color scheme, the glitzy elements aren't overwhelming.

Event Planning | 89

Above and left: The best parts of a design are the details; they express who the host really is. From crystals cascading around a bride's favorite flower and a monogrammed aisle runner to match her custom red cowboy boots to very specific seating plans—the bride wanted guests seated in a theater-in-the-round arrangement—the little details are what guests take away with them when the celebration is over.

Facing page: When the same room is used for the ceremony and the reception, we have to flip it. At The Denver Center for the Performing Arts we made use of the large lobby and mezzanine for a cocktail hour between events. While guests were enjoying the cocktail hour in a separate section of the venue, a seasoned crew completely rearranged everything in the ballroom. Chandeliers were lowered over the tables, drapes were opened to afford guests with views of the Rockies, and flowers that had lined the window wall during the ceremony became centerpieces for the reception tables. Such an undertaking can be done in under an hour, but not without extensive planning beforehand; like every event, these things have to be choreographed like a ballet.

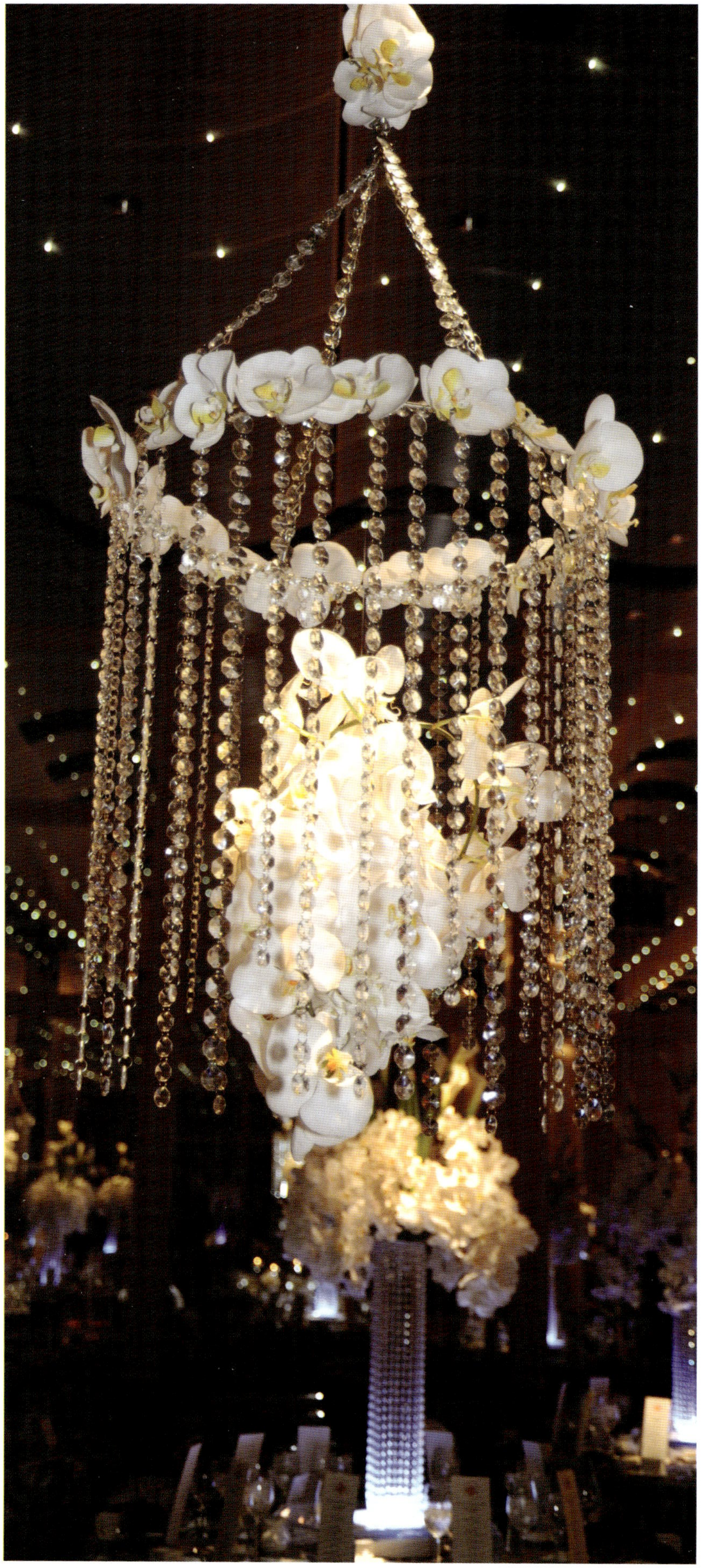

Photograph by Roddie McInnes

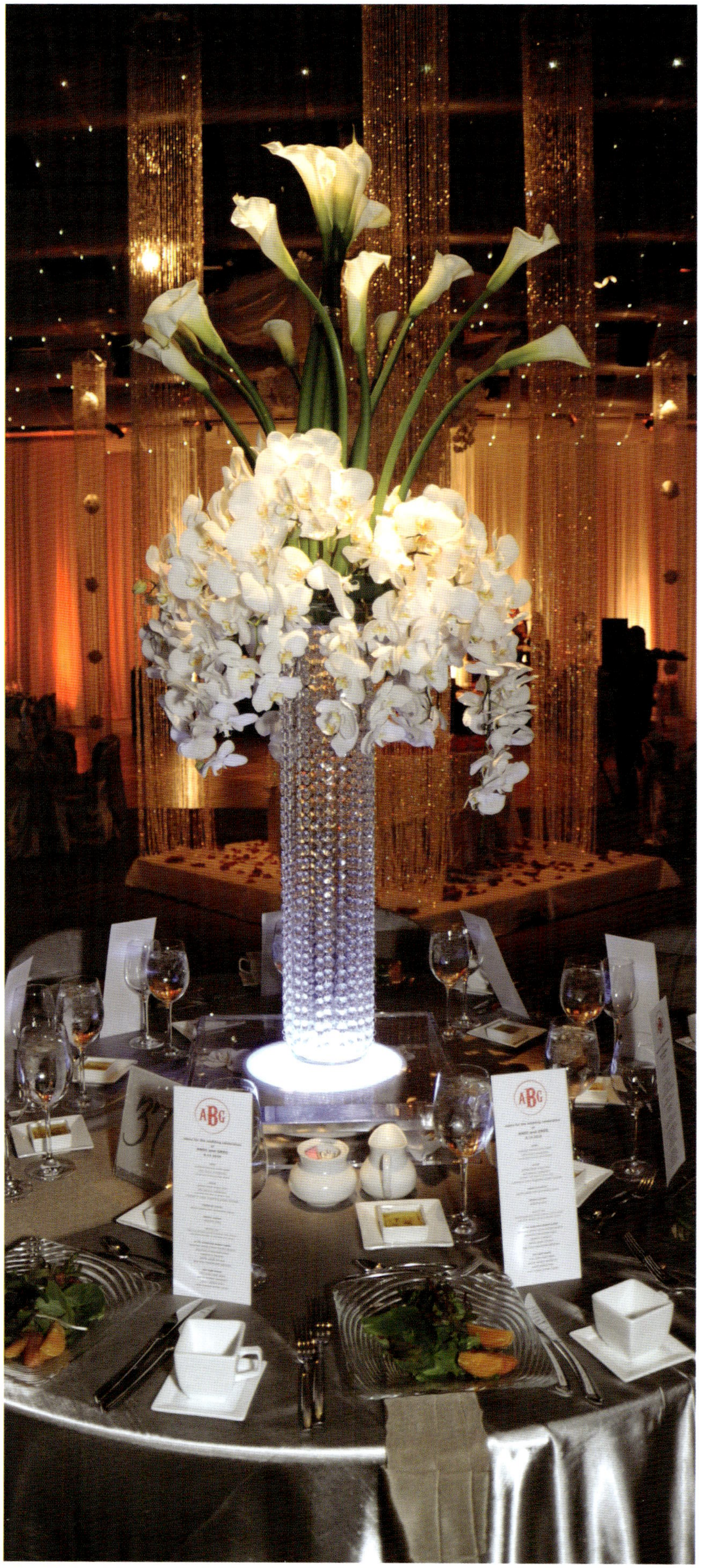

Photograph by Roddie McInnes

Photograph by Andrew Clark

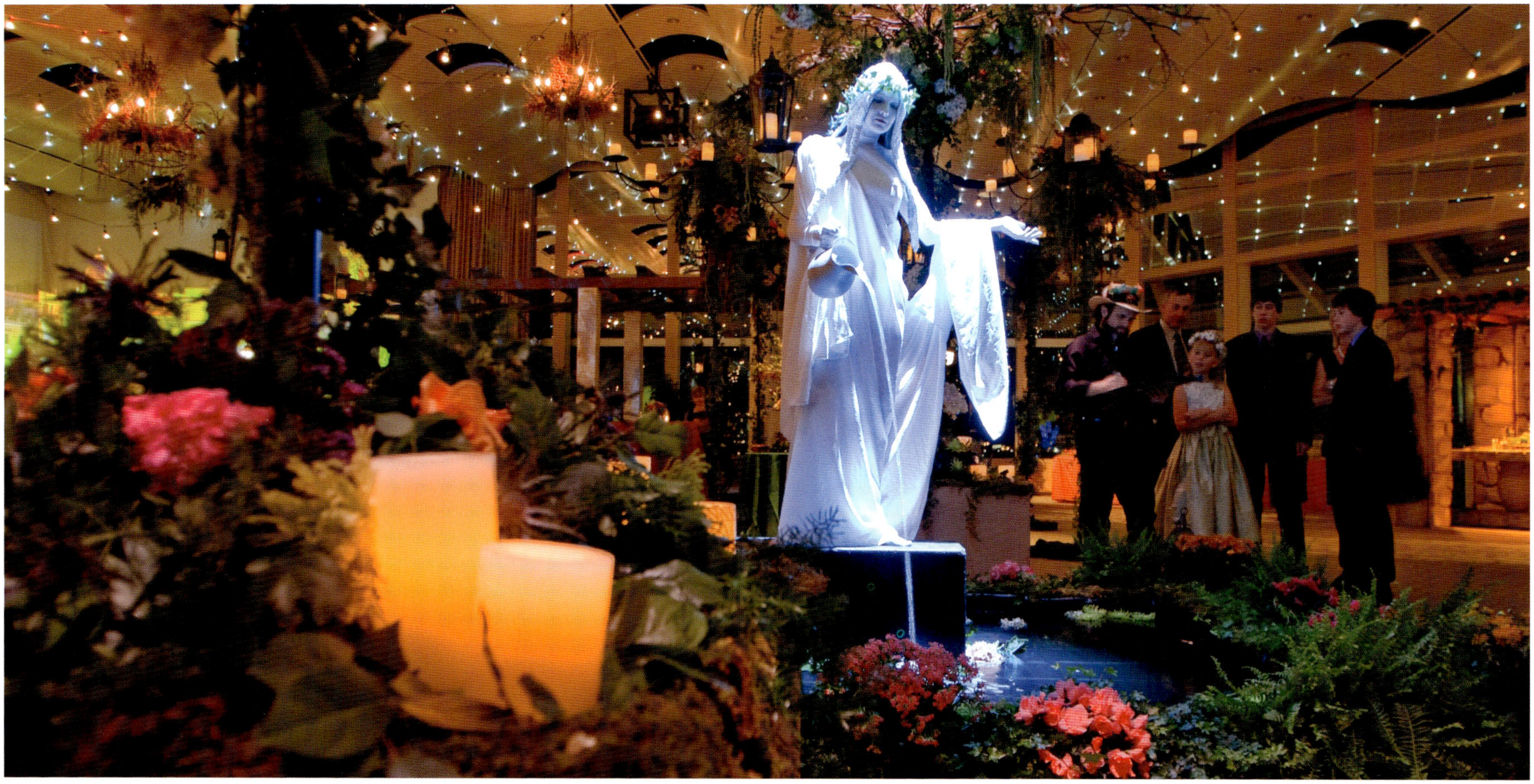

Photograph by Andrew Clark

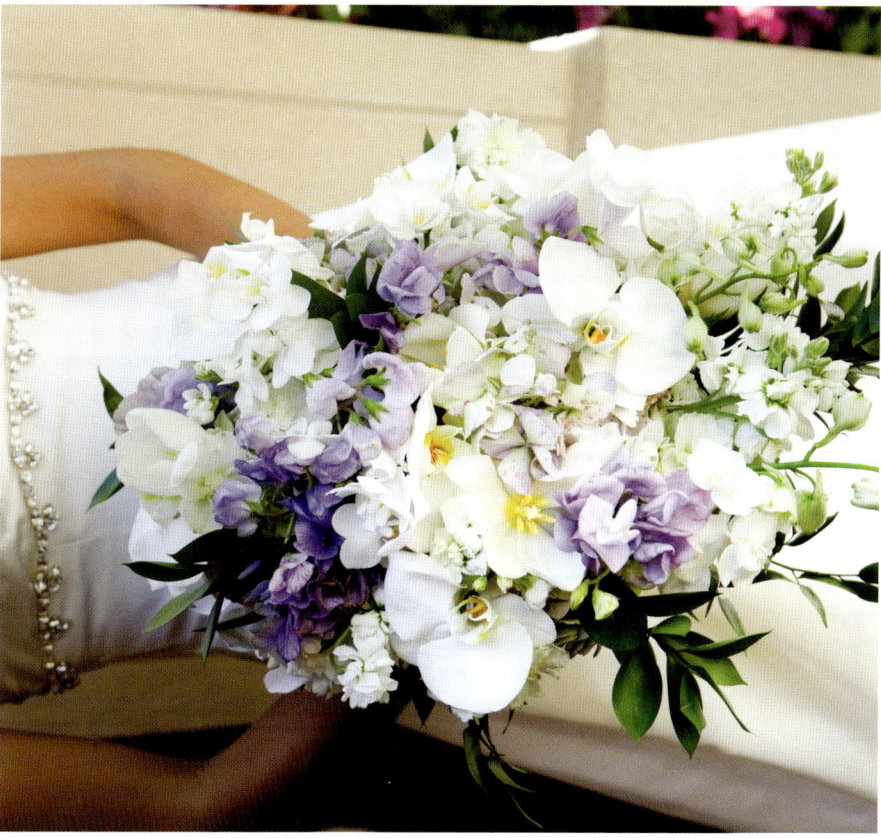

Making someone's dream into a reality sometimes means going to great lengths to find exactly what will set that event apart from everyone else's. For some events, this means shipping gold dinnerware and glassware from California; for others, "live statues" and delicacies from Italy are a must-have. The needs for each event are as varied as their hosts, but going to any length to produce what's been imagined is always worth it.

Photograph by Andrew Clark

Photograph by Andrew Clark

"Every event needs to have some playfulness and whimsy in its design."
—Walli Richardson

When deciding on a theme for your event, it's the little things that really carry the theme to fruition. An Italian village theme was enhanced by the flowering "gardens" and the gondola-shaped bar carved entirely from ice, which held shots of limoncello—a traditional Italian liqueur—and greeted guests upon arrival. The artistic bride and groom's first reception at the Denver Art Museum carried over to their second reception at the Seawell Grand Ballroom. Tiny details like the flower girls' wings—constructed of flowers and flower petals—reminded guests of great Italian artwork and kept the theme consistent.

views

No matter how finely tuned a plan is, something inevitably will turn out differently than you expected. Teaming up with an event planner who makes you feel safe, who encourages you to communicate when things are diverging from the plan, makes all of the difference in the world. Having a comfortable, open-forum relationship with your planner ensures your party will go the way you want it to.

JOHN TOBEY EVENT DESIGN

JOHN TOBEY

Inspired to make things beautiful from a young age, John Tobey has cultivated a reputation for exquisite and heartfelt event design. He garnered his vast experience by working in the service industry for many years before founding EVENTeur, his event design firm, in 2000. Eleven years later, it was rebranded as John Tobey Event Design. John has worked with the likes of Olympian Jeremy Bloom, celebrity event planner Colin Cowie, and even Oprah herself, designing events ranging from grand product launch parties to intimate weddings and everything in between. He has also been honored as the event coordinator for the 2012 ICON Awards Gala.

Dedicating his time to one pro bono charity event per quarter, John has produced numerous soirées in the Denver area. From the Bonded Against Huntington's Disease gala for the Huntington's Disease Society of America—which required an attire dubbed "super spy chic"—to a cocktail party for Freedom Service Dogs, a sweet tribute to Noel Cunningham for The Cunningham Foundation, and a benefit for the Mi Casa Resource Center, John believes in giving back.

In crafting the perfect memories for his hosts, John keeps things as stress-free as possible. He creates "virtual Valium," proclaiming that the only dramatic part of the process should be the event itself. He believes in looking for modern solutions to event planning, such as high-end, eco-friendly electronic invitations for weddings. What it all comes down to, however, is his attitude toward event planning: "Let's have a party."

Light is a very effective element in event design, especially in a modern setting. It can easily be used to break up space or create geometric patterns; it affects the architecture of a room. Setting elements, like centerpieces or the tables themselves, on a diagonal moves a design from traditional to modern.

Event Production | 97

Photograph by Angela Beldy

When designing in an expansive area, crafting small vignettes helps to condense the space so guests don't feel lost in the grandeur. Together with vibrant colors—whether luxurious jewel tones or warm, earthy hues—and strategic lighting, linens provide a fabulous backdrop for an event. Table linens can project a lush feel or create clean lines, and draperies become a canvas for other celebration effects.

"Each event is unique, exquisite, and exceptional."

—John Tobey

Photograph by Chad Chisholm

Photograph by Chad Chisholm

Photograph by Jenna Walker

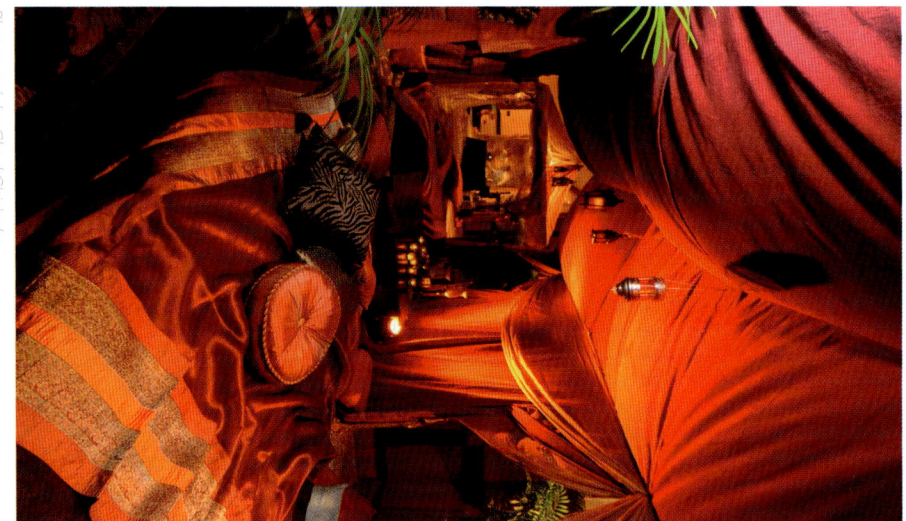

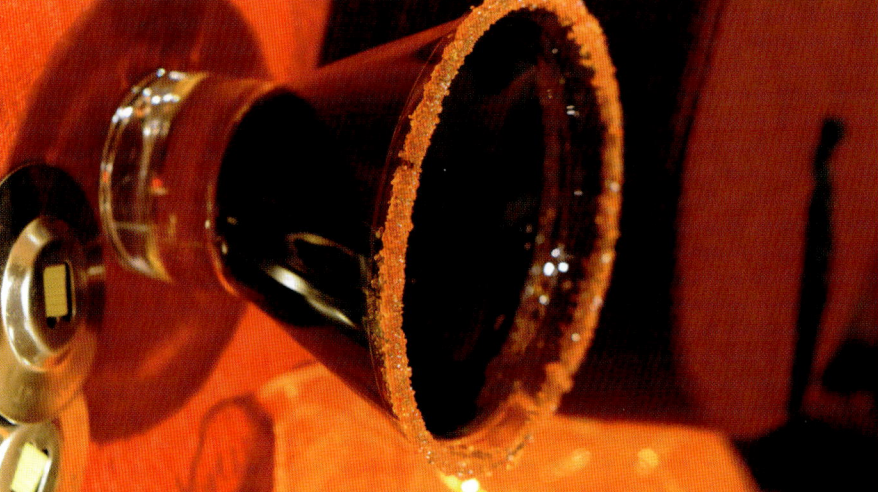

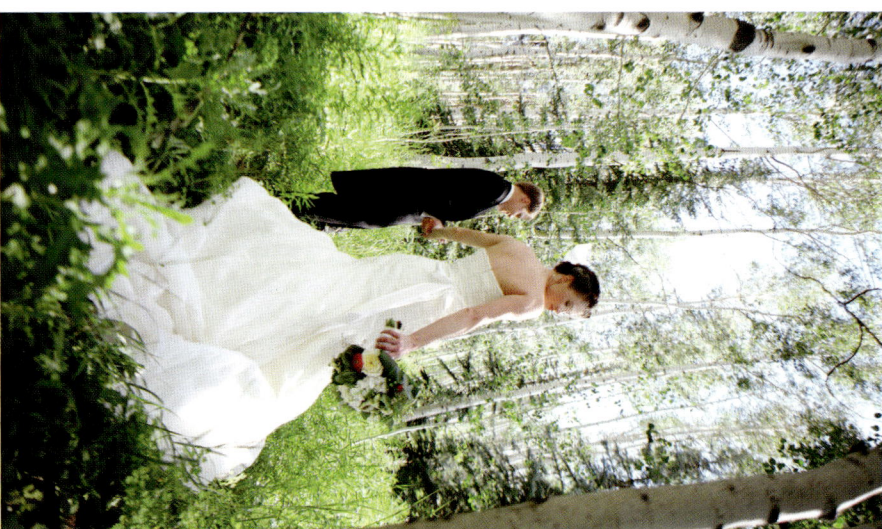

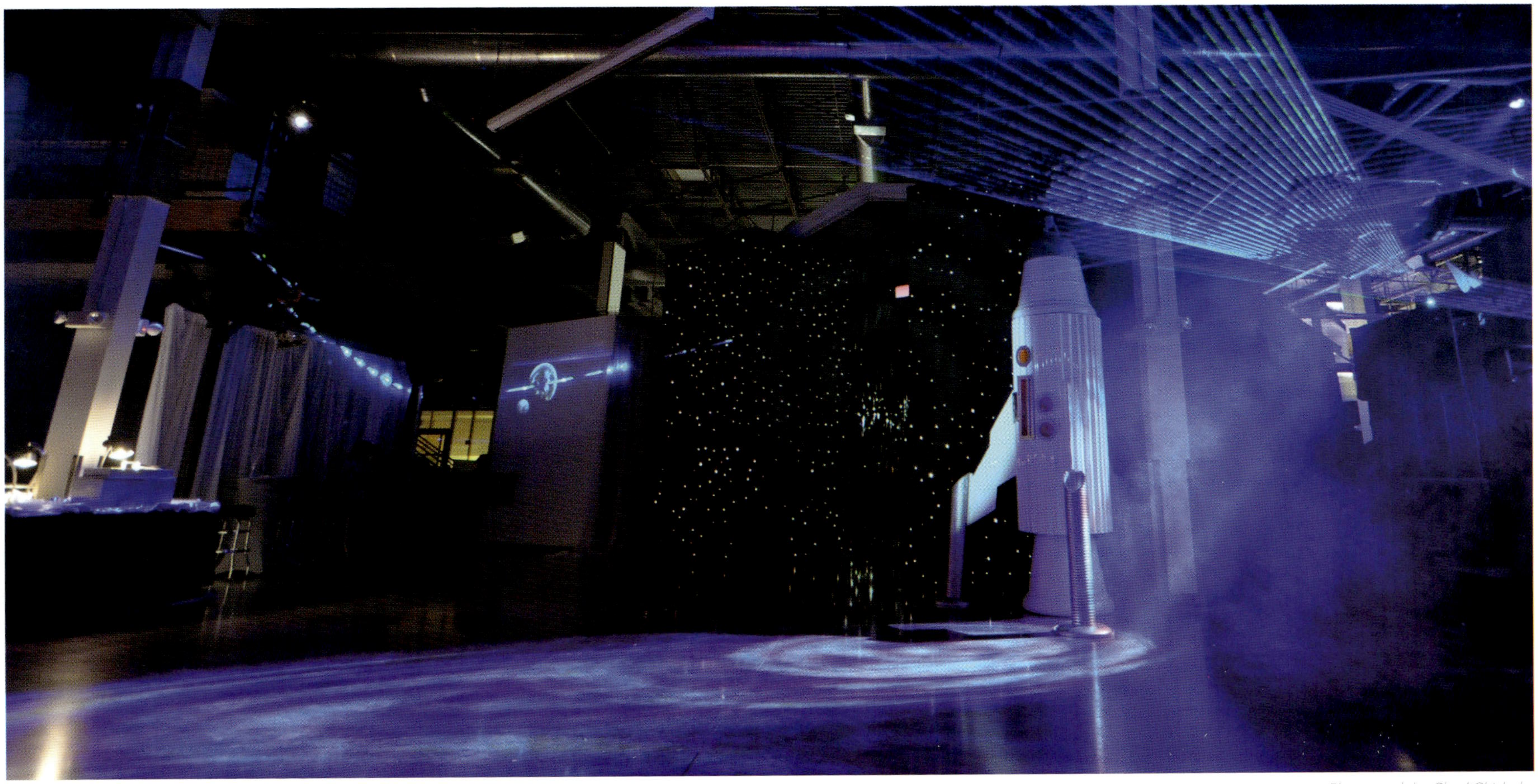

Photograph by Chad Chisholm

Photograph by Steve Peterson

"In memories, the details are what last."

—John Tobey

Whether large or small, attention to detail makes each celebration different from the last. A song dedicated to the newly married couple, a specialty drink, or custom videography all personalize a soirée.

Find an event planner who can make even the smallest celebration a dramatic, elegant affair. The size of the venue or the guest list should not limit the glamour of your event.

views

Kelli Kindel Events

KELLI KINDEL

Getting things right—and making sure the event is stunning—isn't just important for Kelli Kindel and her team, it's essential. And with almost three decades in the event industry, Kelli knows how to ensure success.

Kelli Kindel Events, an event planning firm founded in 1994, represents the culmination of Kelli's valuable knowledge and experience gained through a degree in communications as well as nonprofit and media work. She and her team have become known as a rock-solid group, dedicated to going the extra mile to make each event as incredible as it can be. From unending lists that cover even the smallest detail to six pages of what-if scenarios that involve all the event components, nothing is too small to be included. Kelli also is adept at envisioning the big picture and crafting just the right atmosphere for each event, whether formal or casual, large or intimate, or anything in between.

Kelli's involvement in events such as Governor John Hickenlooper's Inaugural Dinner and Dance is a perfect example of her team's stellar abilities. Not only was the event designed for thousands of attendees—a feat in and of itself—but a layer of ice existed on the streets around the venue just four hours before guests were to arrive. So Kelli and a few other brave souls used ice picks and shovels to clear the street and parking lot for the valet, living out their unspoken motto that nothing will stand in the way of a successful celebration. Situations like this prove that Kelli Kindel Events is an indispensible part of planning an event.

At Lulu's Barkin' BBQ, a premier summer fundraiser for the Dumb Friends League, we used simple, elegant floral centerpieces combined with canvas bag favors touting the nonprofit's logo to ensure the setting was beautiful and fiscally responsible. They also kept guests focused on the real reason for the party: the organization's mission of helping homeless pets.

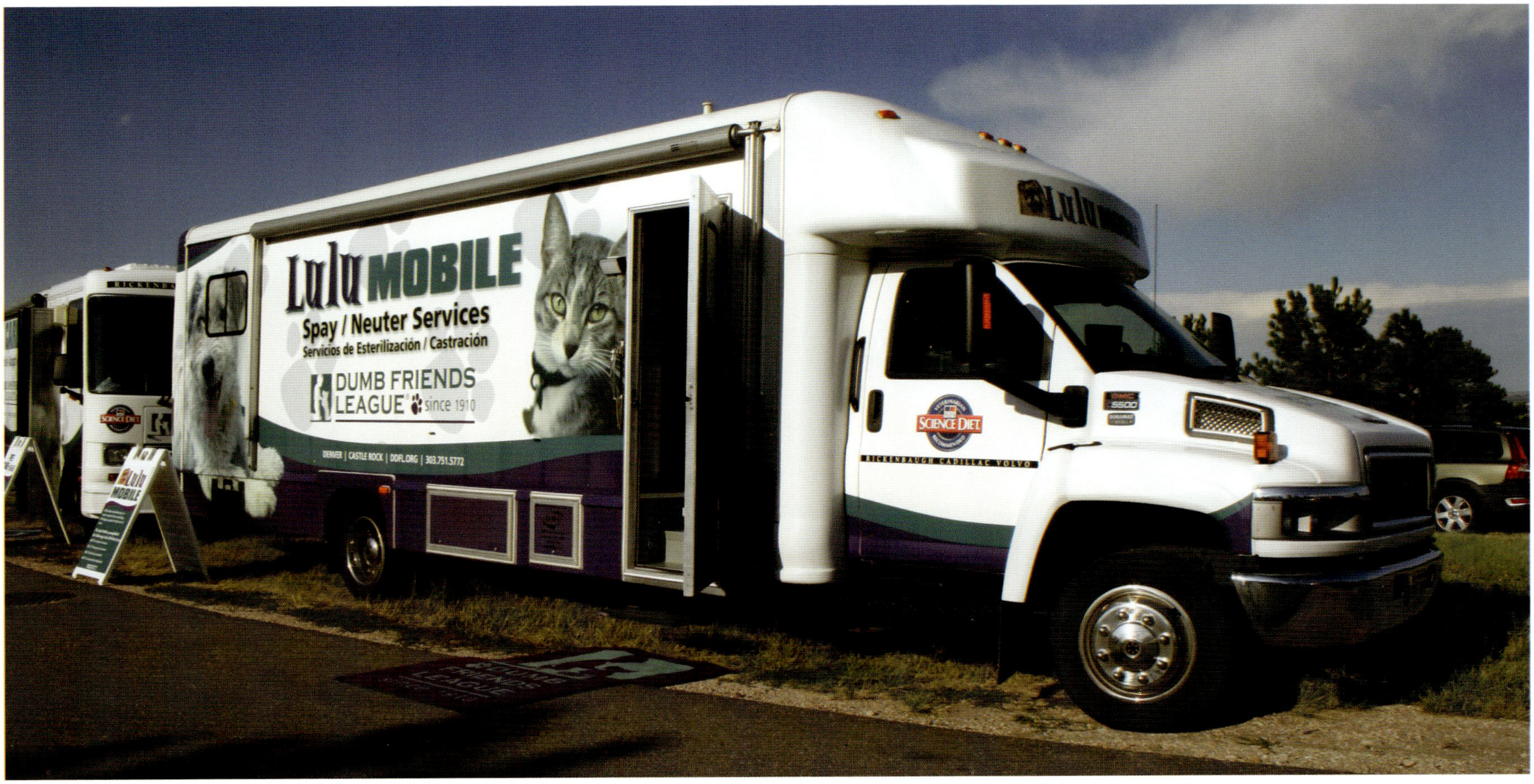

Photograph courtesy of the Dumb Friends League

Photograph courtesy of the Dumb Friends League

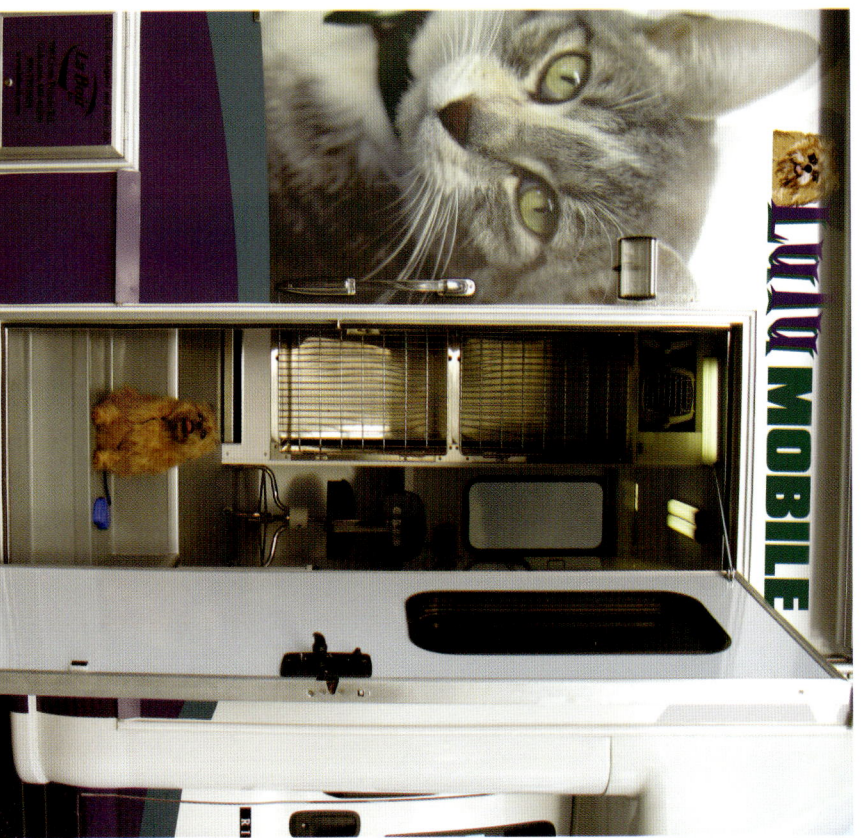

The Dumb Friends League event, which brings 500 guests to the Castle Pines home of Jana and Fred Bartlit, is all about having fun and highlighting the organization and services it provides. Surrounding the tents, we brought in the League's mobile outreach units containing many adorable cats and dogs that were available for adoption throughout the evening. Inside the tent, we created an incredible atmosphere with lighting, color, and minimal décor, again respecting the need for fiscal responsibility.

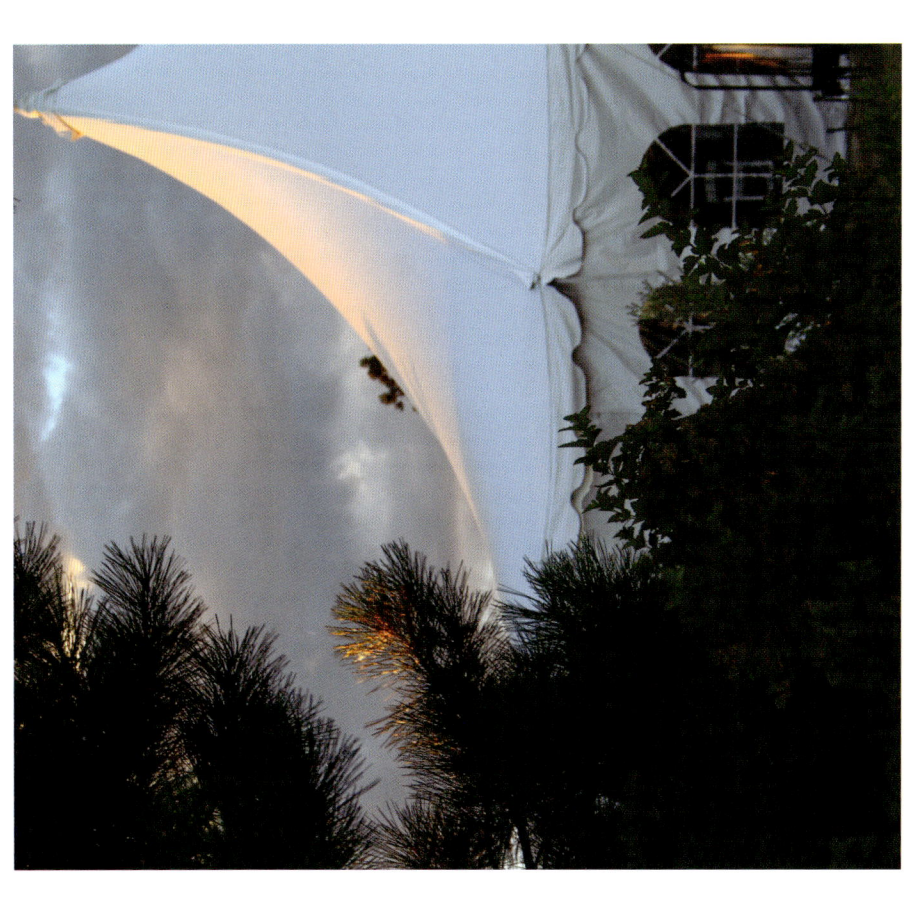

"Each event needs a wow factor to make it stand out from the 15 others held that night."

—Kelli Kindel

Photograph courtesy of the Dumb Friends League

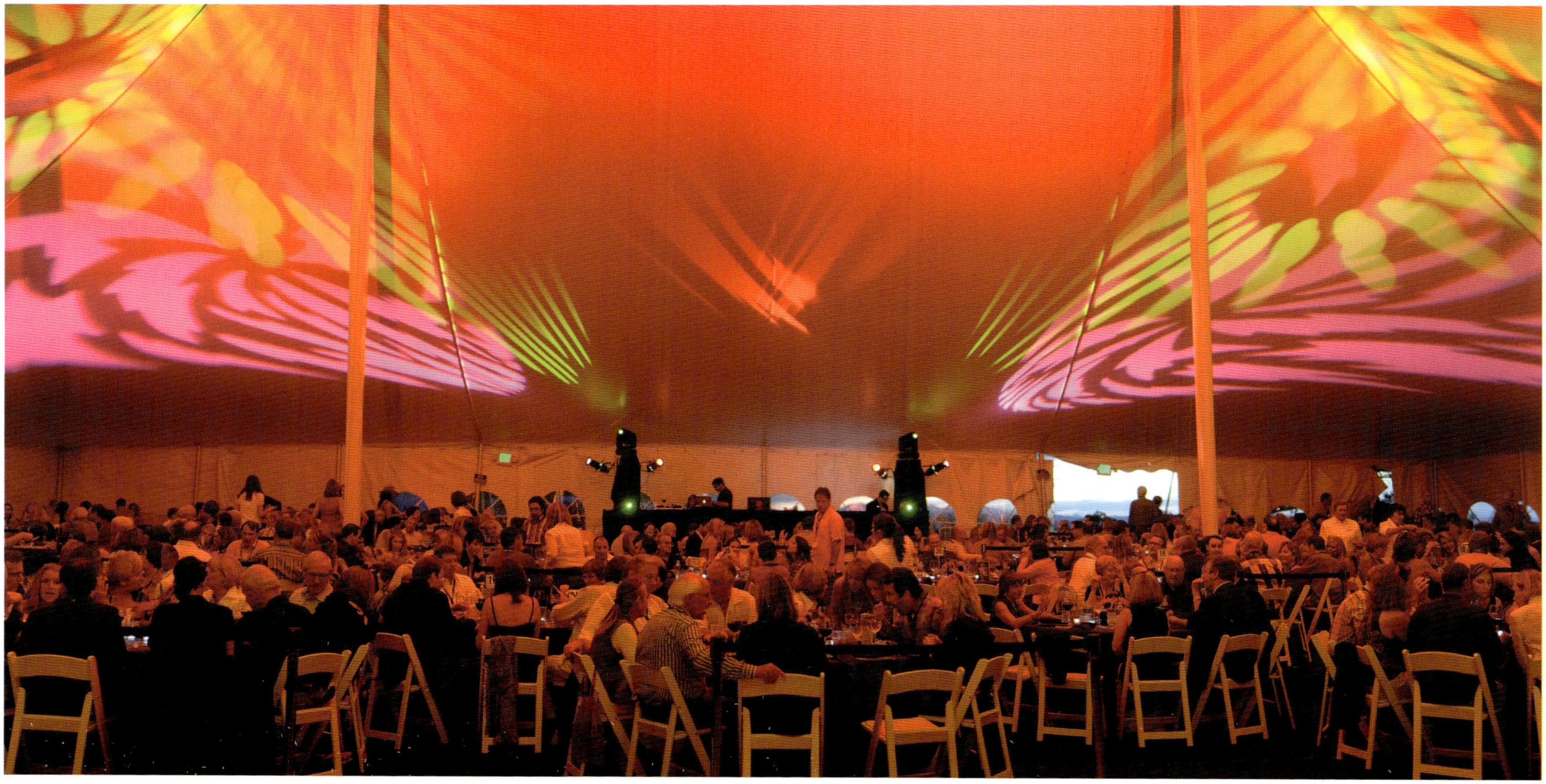

Photograph courtesy of the Dumb Friends League

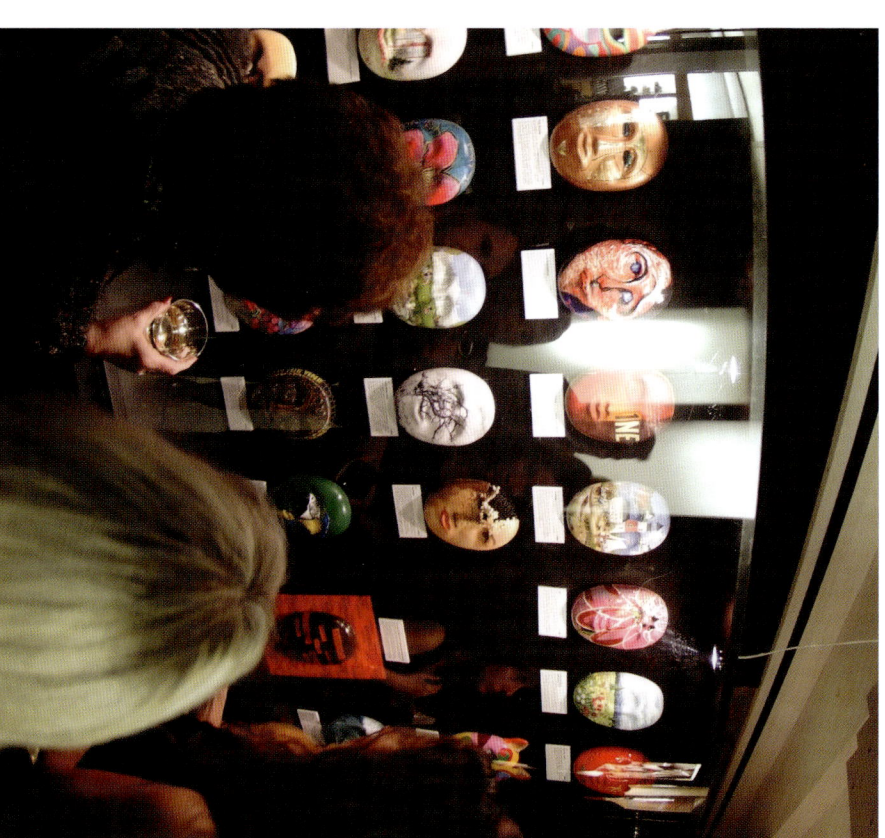

Photograph by Stevie Crecelius, WonderWorks Studios

"Double-checking details is never enough for us; we always triple- or quadruple-check everything."
—Kelli Kindel

Produced as a fundraiser for The Denver Hospice in partnership with Cherry Creek Shopping Center, The Mask Project is a charity art auction featuring hundreds of masks created by celebrities, sports figures, politicians, artists, and recognized members of the community. We were ecstatic to help with such a wonderful event, which runs for about four weeks so the public can view the masks. We helped organize the finale events, which included a fashion show with models and firefighters, guest speakers, and auction, for 1,000 people, with only about one and a half hours to set up after mall hours, a task that normally takes a full day.

views

Always put yourself in the guest's seat. You should strive to make the event fun and memorable, so that guests leave the party saying, "Wow! That was one of the most fun events I have ever attended."

PUTTIN' ON THE RIZZ

RICHARD W. RIZZO

Richard W. Rizzo, founder of Puttin' on the RIZZ, has a goal for each event he's involved in: simple elegance. Subtle guidance and unpretentious design are also hallmarks of Richard's work, and since establishing his event coordination firm in 2009, he has proven time and again to be a versatile and skilled personal event concierge. Richard is sensitive and accommodating to every budget and need any host may have—he wants the event to be perfect in every way. Regardless of size or occasion, Richard puts his heart and soul into each celebration; he treats hosts like members of his own family.

During his tenure as executive vice president of Epicurean Catering, Richard had an uncompromising and unwavering commitment to excellence in creating memorable events. That conviction has continued with Puttin' on the RIZZ. With an understanding that the events he coordinates represent the most important moments in a person's life, Richard continually educates himself on the latest trends and sacred traditions of his clientele, such as the strict guidelines of kosher cuisine. Absolutely no detail is too small for Richard to devote his attention to; if it is significant to a host, it is significant to him.

From social gatherings, weddings, and mitzvahs to large-scale corporate, political, and sporting events, Richard is ready for any challenge, even offering "day of" coordination. In addition to private soirées, he has also participated in functions for the NBA All Star Weekend, Denver Broncos Football Club, and The INTERNATIONAL at Castle Pines Golf Club. Repeatedly nominated for ICON Awards in numerous categories, Richard was even honored with coordinating the organization's 2010 and 2011 awards ceremony. When asked to explain what he does for a living, Richard's response flawlessly sums up his outlook: "I make perfect."

Creating intimate spaces for a reception brings guests together in a personal way and really makes the event memorable.

Photograph by Stevie Crecelius, WonderWorks Studios

"Where emotions are heightened, memories are inevitable."

—Richard W. Rizzo

Photograph by Stevie Crecelius, WonderWorks Studios

Pops of color and light bring vibrancy to any space. Whether that color comes in the form of lime sorbet-colored linens and luscious floral arrangements or as hundreds of lights strung against the night sky or shot into the air, color electrifies an event with energy.

Photograph by Andrew Clark Photography

views

"Possibilities are endless."
—Richard W. Rizzo

Celebrations are fun; elements like décor, cuisine, and entertainment should reflect this basic concept. When touches of whimsy in the form of ice sculptures, live statues, or sumptuous buffets are added, the event automatically takes on a new dimension.

Work with a coordinator who advises without bias, recommends without thoughts of personal gain, and respects your expectations. It is, after all, your event and not theirs.

WM Events

WILLIAM FOGLER

Event planning and design are hardwired into William Fogler's DNA. Growing up in a household where every occasion was decorated and celebrated, he found his passion early. Over the past two decades, his professional career has taken him from catering server to founder and creative director of WM Events, a full-service event planning and design firm with offices in Denver and Atlanta. Since its launch in 2004, William and his team have assembled an impressive portfolio of high-end events for a broad range of clientele at a multitude of venues.

Relying on his keen eye for the aesthetic, logistical prowess, and limitless energy, William is dedicated to offering the highest caliber of services encompassing all aspects of an event. Empowered by the belief that he is entrusted with shaping and executing a once-in-a-lifetime moment, nothing is left to chance. One detail at a time from color, texture, sound, and taste, a sensational celebration takes shape. Whether it is an extravagant wedding, charity fundraiser, private party, or corporate function, events are highly reflective of the host's sensibilities so as to create a palpable sense of identity and intention.

It is easy to understand why so many of his clientele remain lifelong friends—his effervescent personality is tempered with a breath of benevolence and a dose of the commonsensical that quickly builds rapport and instills trust. William's hands-on, partnership-style approach means he is there every step of the way, from initial conception and storyboarding to hitting the lights and fluffing the train.

Pastures of Plenty, a 35-acre organic vegetable, herb, and flower farm outside Boulder, is a rustic, earthy venue for exchanging vows. To balance the pastoral feel of the farm, we designed a classic, heirloom-adorned tablescape replete with custom-made linens, antique china, and silverware from the family collection. Chipboard frames with a photo of each guest were a unique twist on seating assignments. Anchoring the table and adding a punch of color and drama are vibrant sprays of fresh-cut flowers and statuesque candelabras. The results are romantic, warm, and oh-so-elegant.

Event Planning | 115

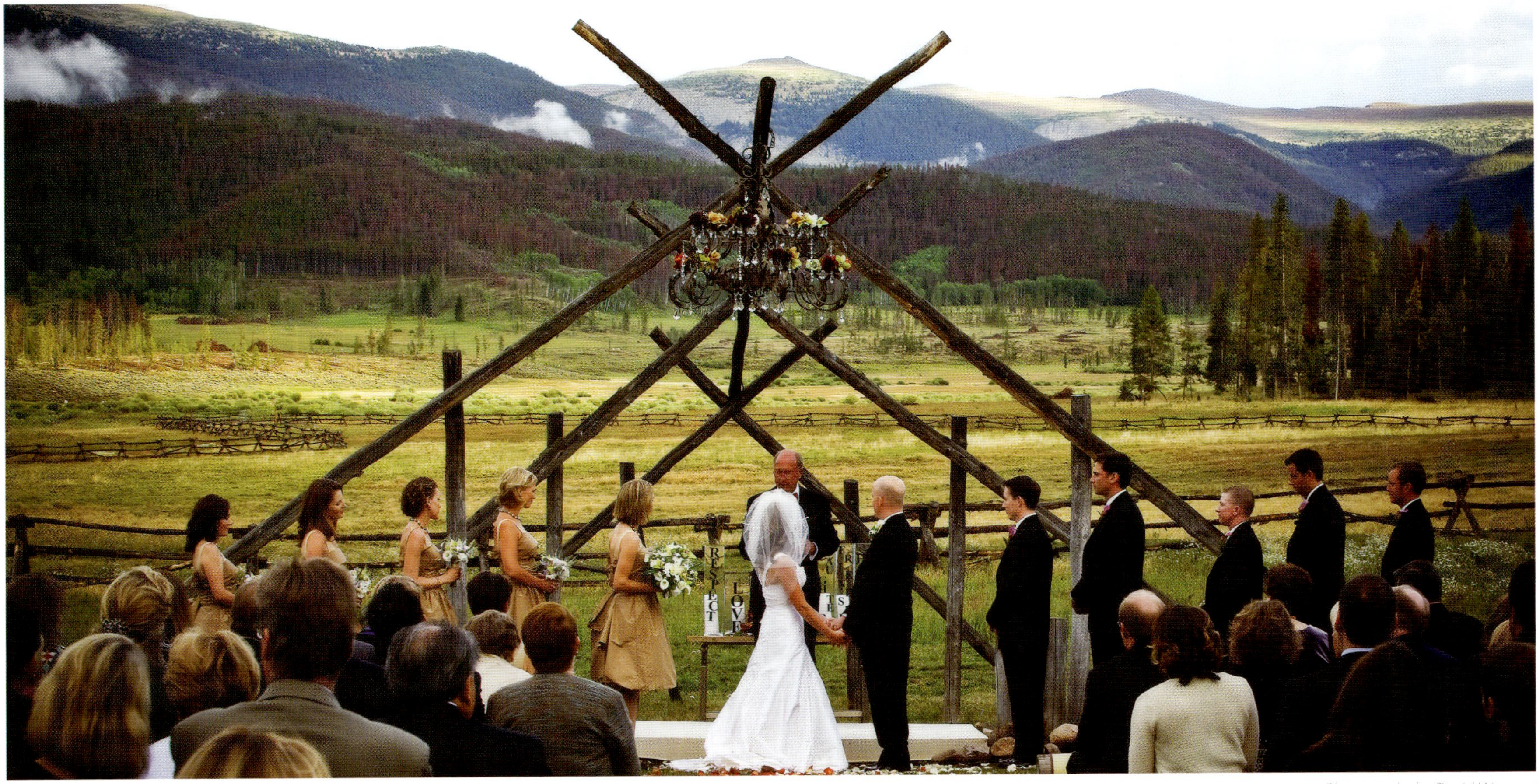

Photographs by David Wegwart

Photograph by Patrick Williams

Photographs by David Wegwart

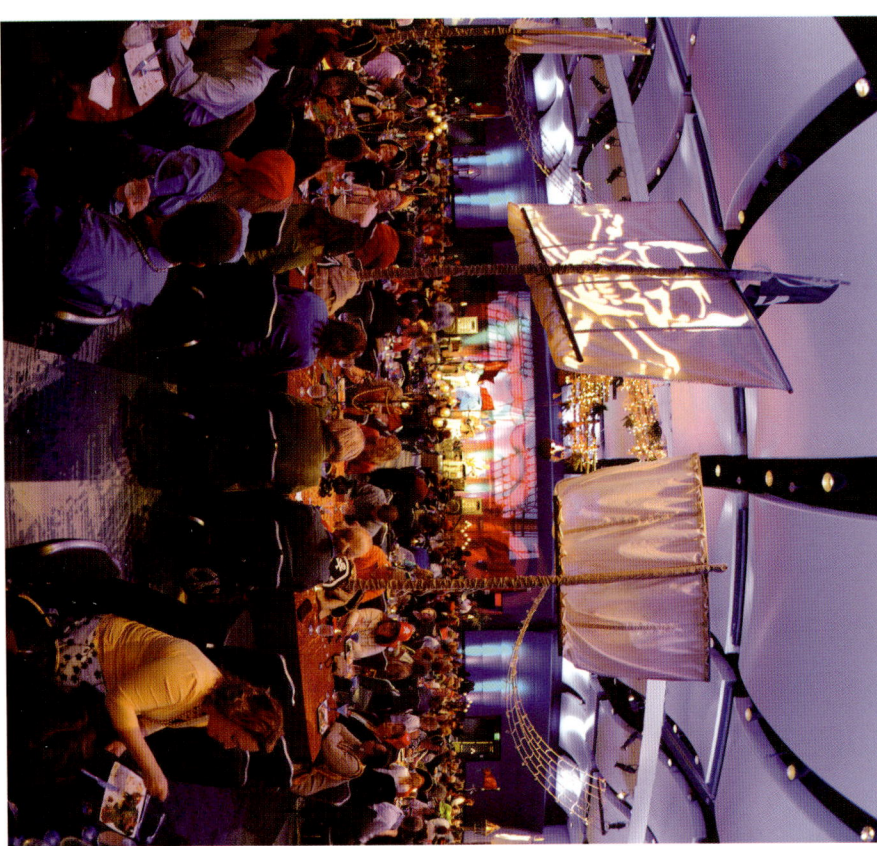

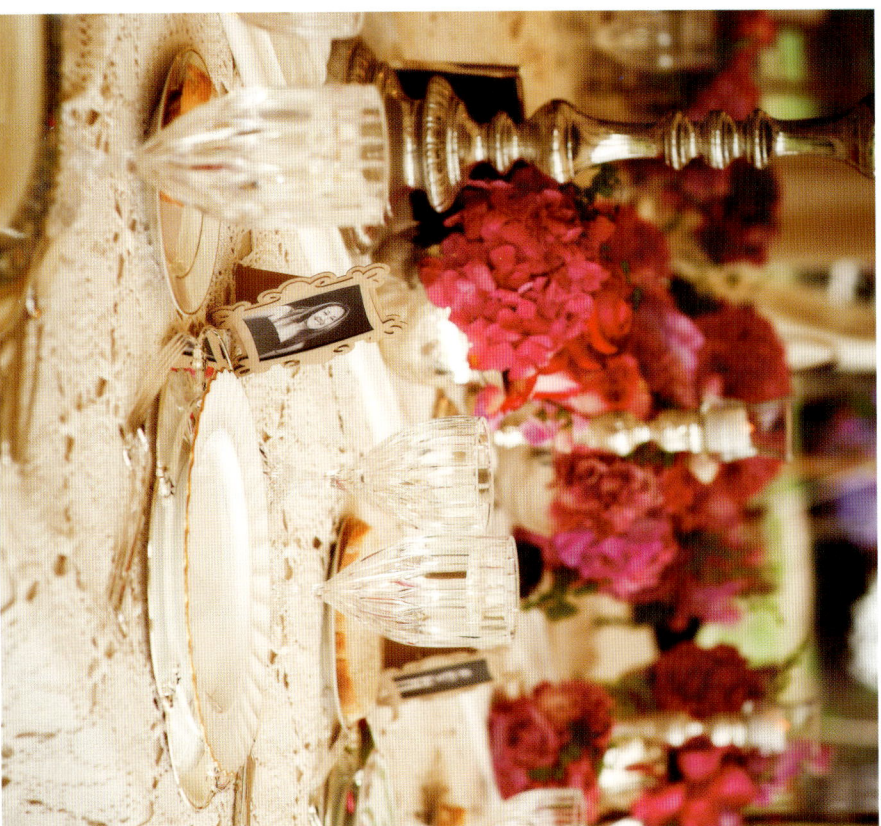

SANCTUARY
BRAD THOMPSON

When looking for a venue with a stunning setting and impeccable service, look no further than Sanctuary, an exclusive golf course and clubhouse that opens its facilities for social events to those in the community and out-of-town guests.

Hosting events since 1997, the team members are certainly not newcomers to creating and executing unbelievable soirées. Matching the level of unbelievable views of flora, fauna, and mountains, they operate on the philosophy that every need must be met before the guest even realizes the need, and it must all be accomplished subtly. The team members also understand the importance of attention to detail and undivided focus. They only schedule one event at a time, and they create a master plan that is followed by three managers who are onsite during every event.

Carefully placed on a beautiful ecosystem with more than 12,400 surrounding acres of dedicated open space, Sanctuary has become a place of respite from the hustle and bustle of Denver, which is only minutes away. The great care that the team members put into every event is evidence that they take pride in making sure every host and guest enjoys that ambience too.

Views from our spacious clubhouse include majestic towering pines and stunning panoramic sight lines from Pikes Peak to Longs Peak.

Location

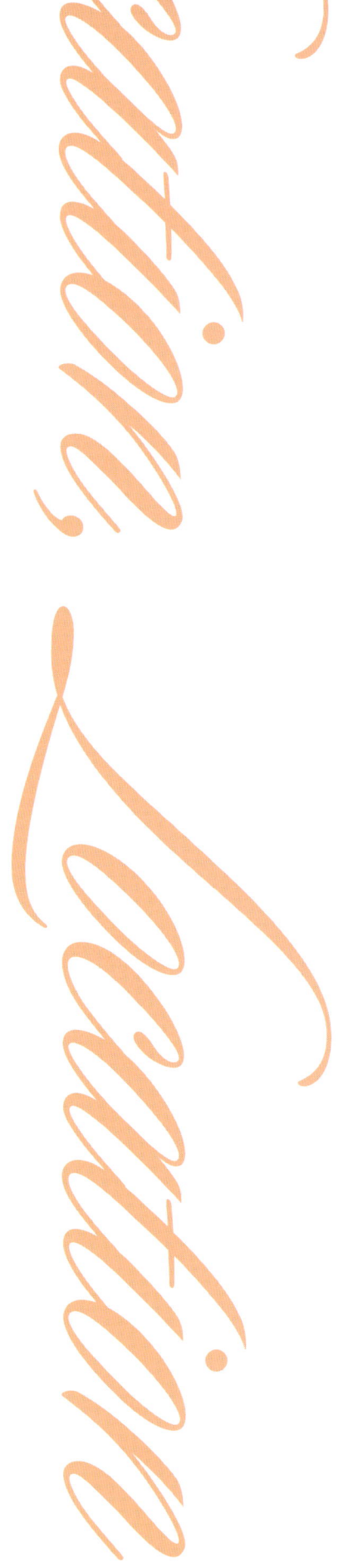

Location

Photograph by Adam Frazier, Artistic Imaging

"Planning the party should be just as much fun as the party itself."
—William Fogler

It's all about creative versatility and vision. From organic nuptials to themed corporate events to contemporary soirées, our events run the gamut, with the commonality being that they are each inspired by individuals with unique personalities and expressions of style. Our overreaching goal is to take a concept—however raw or refined, opulent or austere—and elicit those subtle nuances and rarefied details that will ultimately define the event. Then we collaboratively refine the vision and hone the minutiae until a one-of-a-kind celebration finds form in reality.

views

The objective of an event should be creating lasting memories rather than flaunting excess and overlooking the true meaning of the occasion. Be an excellent host, and your guests will leave with lasting, fond memories of time well spent.

Photograph by Van Buren Photography

Above and facing page bottom: The pavilion, which can seat up to 250 people, is a great place for our guests to enjoy the outdoors while still being protected from the elements. The versatile space gives us the flexibility to utilize the gorgeous mountains as the background or reverse the design for the elegant fireplace to become the backdrop. Both options create just the right ambience, whether day or night.

Facing page top: An especially romantic ambience, further enhanced by our stone gas fireplaces, begins to appear as dusk settles outside the clubhouse's Great Room, where 200 people can be comfortably seated for dinner.

Photograph by broxtonArt

Photograph by broxtonArt

Photograph by broxtonArt

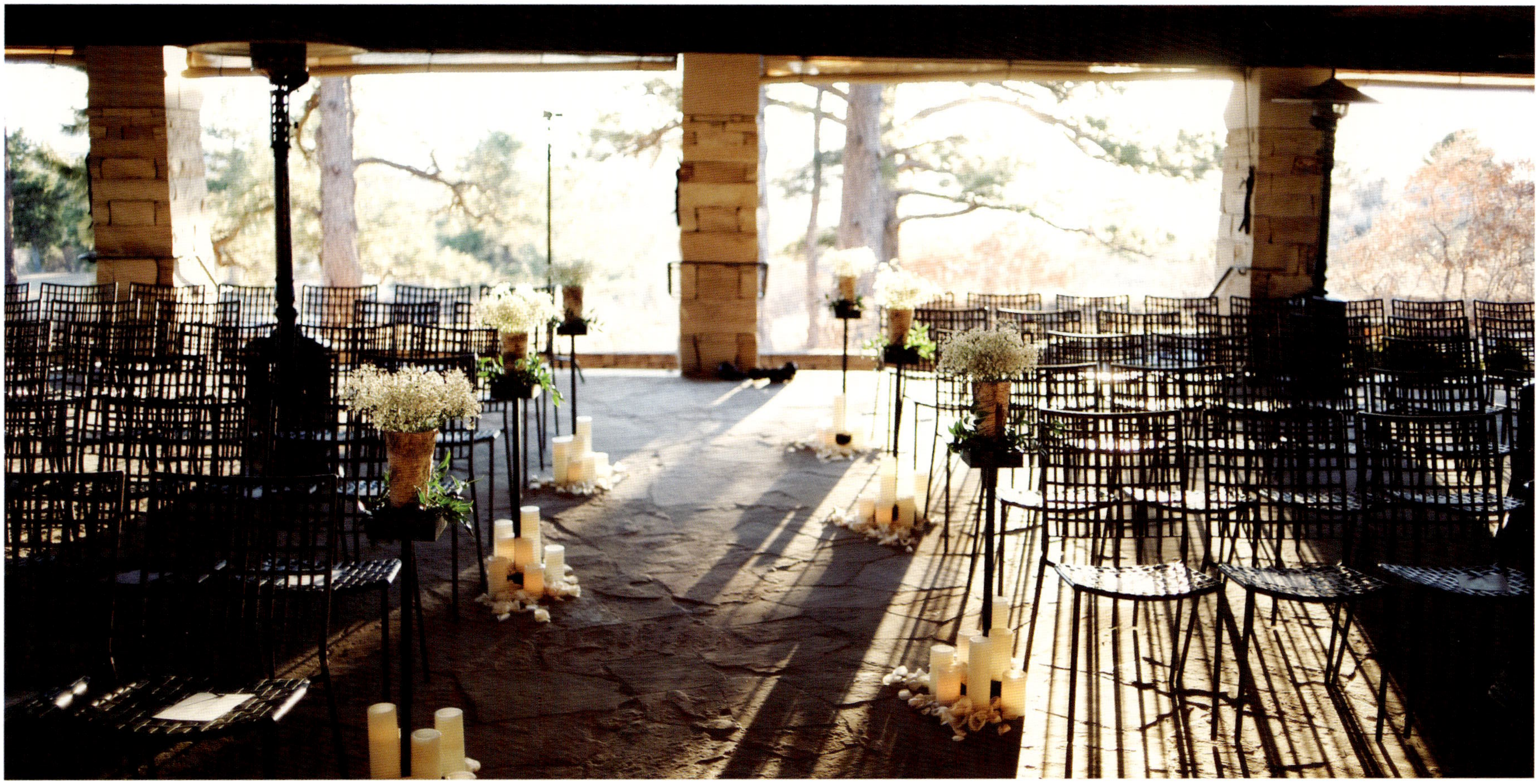

Photograph by Brinton Studios

Photograph by Van Buren Photography

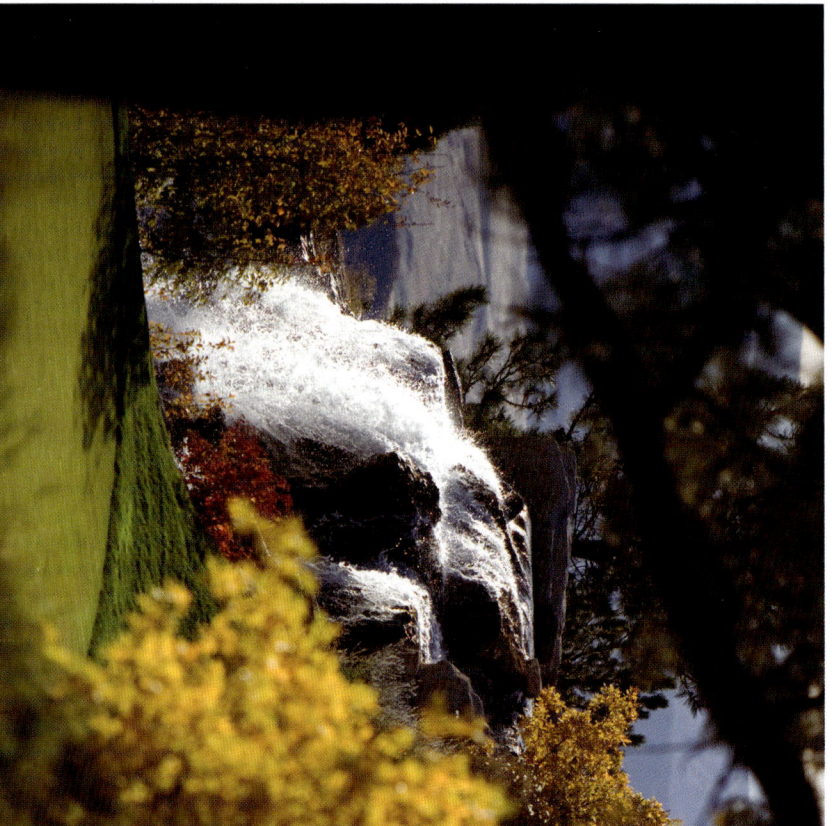

Above: When it's cold outside, we can drop the side panels around the pavilion and bring in heaters to ensure everyone's comfortable while still allowing the beauty of nature to infuse every aspect of the event.

Left and facing page: Other spaces in and around the clubhouse continue the elegant, natural tone, from the picture-perfect waterfall behind hole 9 to the lovely locker room and the grotto walkway that leads up to the pavilion.

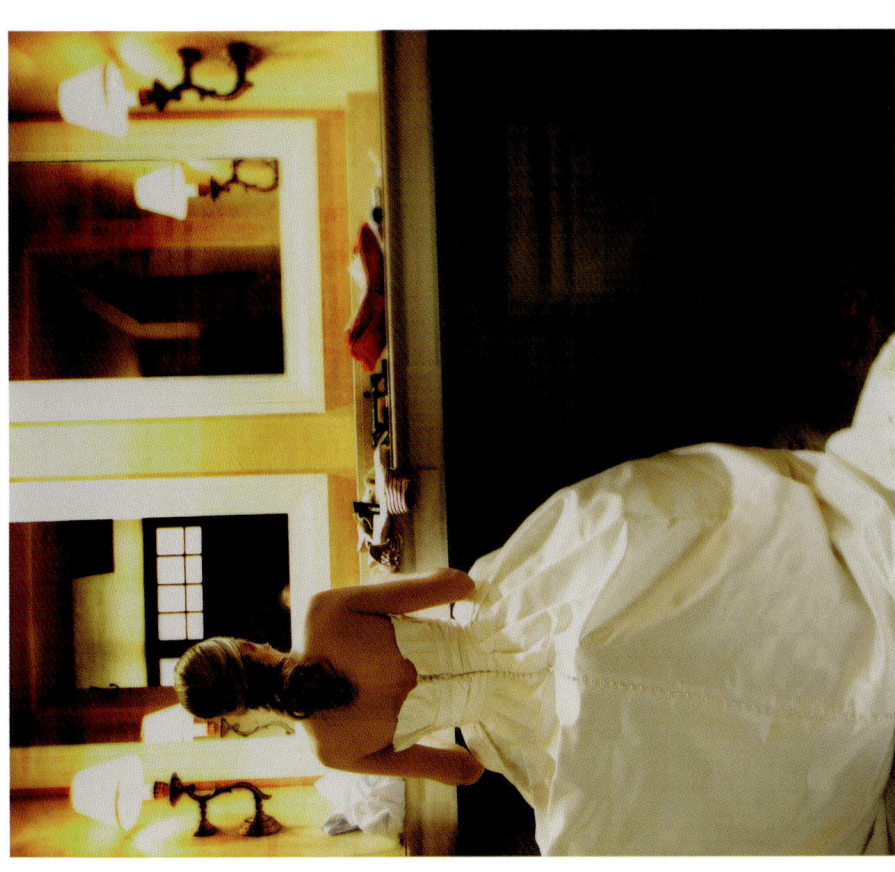

"When the setting is so breathtaking, it really does feel like you've stepped into a world of your own."
—Brad Thompson

Photograph by Brinton Studios

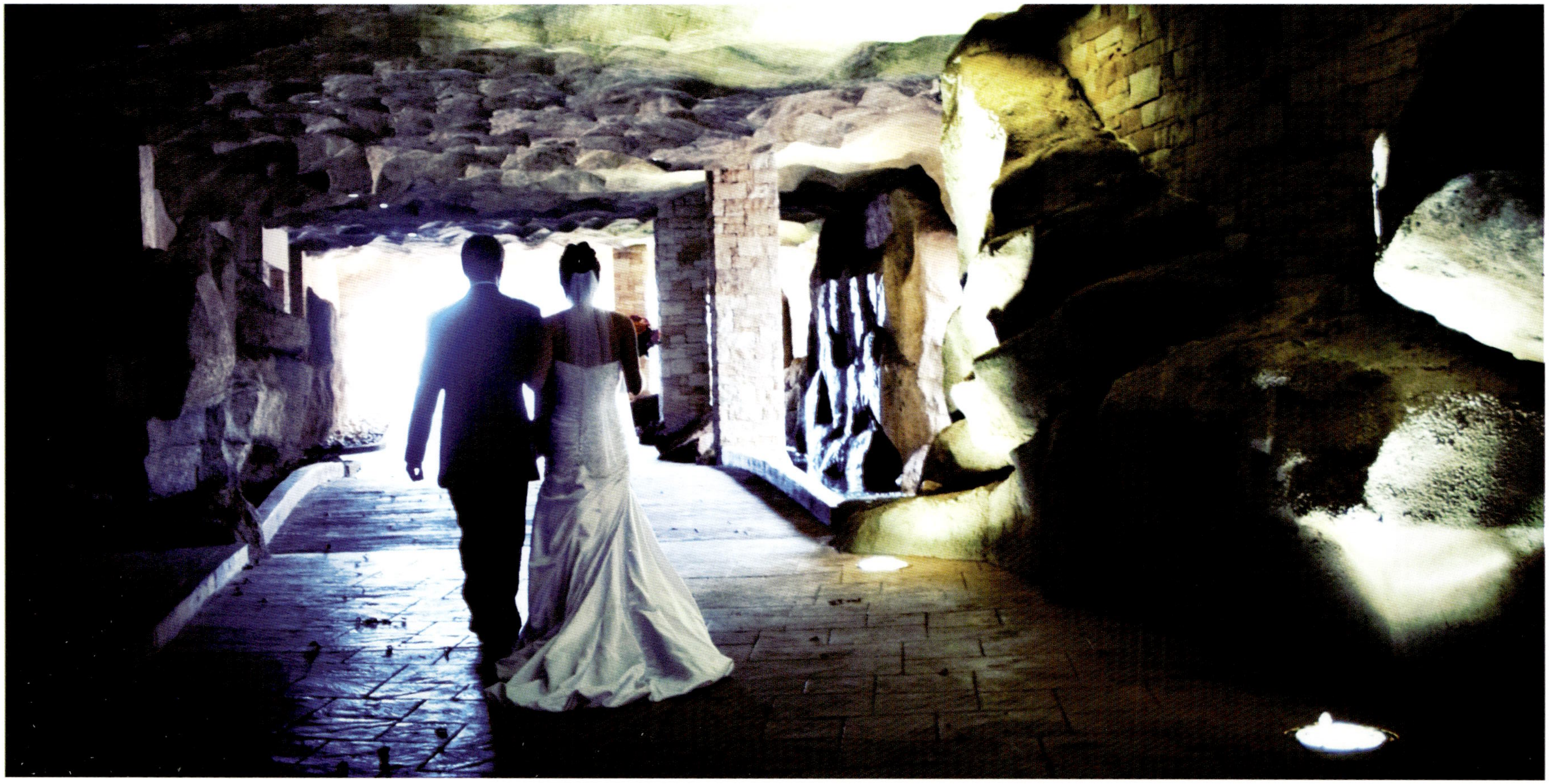

Photograph by broxtonArt

Photograph by Brinton Studios

Above: The grand entrance sets the stage for every event, providing a sense of magnificence as guests arrive. We provide complimentary valet, and a porte-cochère connects the drive to the clubhouse and pavilion so weather won't dampen any event.

Facing page: Our team gets so excited to see every little detail come together, and our master plan ensures that it all comes together perfectly.

"We don't just stop at the expected but go the extra mile to ensure nothing spoils the event; that's what true service means to us."

—Brad Thompson

Art of Celebration | 128

Photograph by broxtonArt

Photograph by broxtonArt

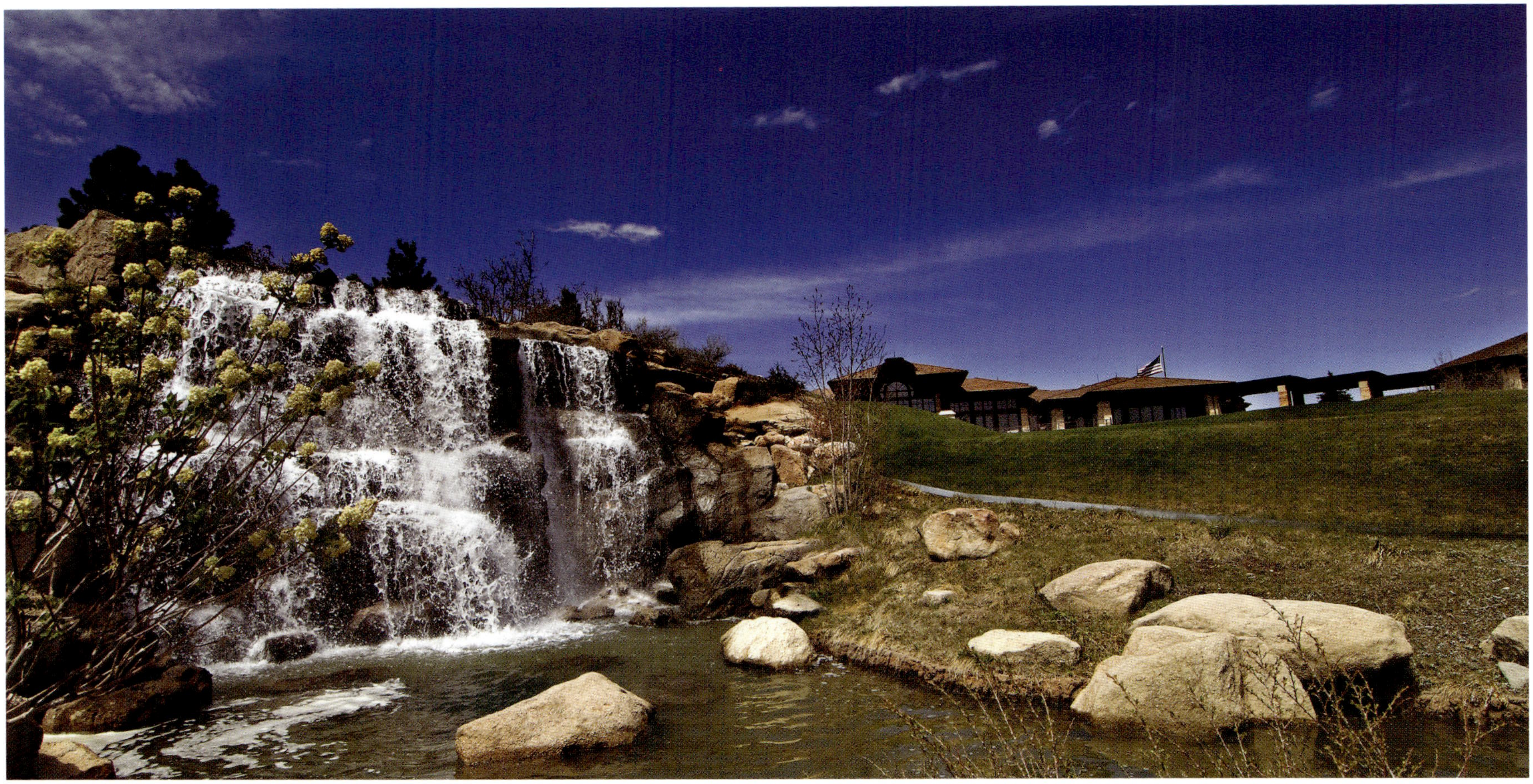

Photograph by broxtonArt

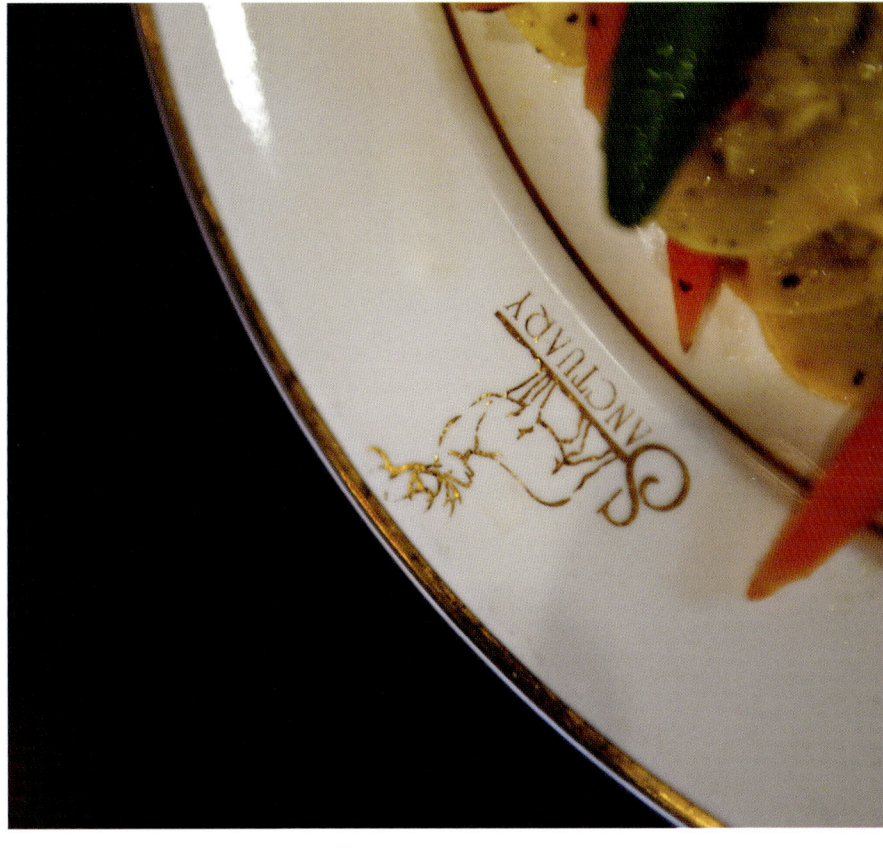

Above and facing page: From a ceremony in the warm, intimate pavilion to photos out by the waterfall to a reception in the light-infused Great Room, we have seen how any style works beautifully with the natural elements.

Right: Our onsite, full-service catering team includes classically trained culinary chefs and skilled banquet staff who know how to successfully execute first-class preparation and presentation.

Photograph by broxtonArt

Right: We often recommend hosts take advantage of the beautiful Colorado native sandstone and exquisite chandeliers that grace the property; one favorite spot for photos is the hallway along the front of the building.

Facing page: The terrace along the rear of the clubhouse is a perfect locale for cocktail hour. Guests can take advantage of heaters on chilly nights and mingle while our servers pass hors d'oeuvres before the real party begins.

views

Selecting a venue should be more than just choosing a pretty location and agreeing with the cost. You'll know you've found the ideal site when you can imagine your perfect event there, and all the other requirements—outstanding service, beautiful setting, etc.—fall into place too.

DELLA TERRA MOUNTAIN CHATEAU

Perched above the cozy mountain town of Estes Park, Della Terra Mountain Chateau is a breathtaking Colorado fantasy. Located just past the Fall River entrance to Rocky Mountain National Park, the property's natural beauty and expertly executed design create the perfect, secluded mountain wedding, retreat, or meeting venue.

Amid the evergreens, stone, and timber, Della Terra offers unsurpassed venues for indoor and outdoor weddings. The happy couple can choose to tie the knot in the elegant Celebration Place, an indoor ceremony and reception area with lofty ceilings, balcony overlooks, and high-arching windows framing mountain views. Alternately, the more intimate Gathering Place epitomizes coziness with its balconies and large fireplaces. Couples who want to say "I do" alfresco fall for the outdoor Devotion Place, a woodsy ceremony area nestled among the pines and offset by the breathtaking backdrop of MacGregor Mountain, where guests take in the ceremony from a terraced hillside.

After the day's activities, guests can reminisce around the Lodge Room's Old World stone fireplace, retreat to the Essence Place for a spa treatment, enjoy an espresso, watch a movie, or hang out in the private hot tub on the balcony of their luxury suite.

Colorado natives Darell and Pam Amelang, Marty and Audrey Miller, and Sandy Garcia developed these 14 forested acres to be as eco-friendly as they are guest-friendly. Creeks, ponds, a stone bridge, secret gazebo, and tiered seating honor the landscape, while solar, high-efficiency, and LED systems save thousands of watts of electricity. With a combined vision and love of nature, this team brings casual elegance to the Colorado mountainside.

Our guests love the chateau's secluded mountain setting. The property has the distinction of being bordered by Rocky Mountain National Park, and the views of the Continental Divide through the aspen trees are truly spectacular.

Photograph courtesy of Taylor Adam Swift

Photograph courtesy of Dreamtime Images

"Choose a venue that hosts only one wedding at a time. When a facility keeps the spotlight on you alone, the results become richer, more intimate, and unforgettable."

—Pam Amelang

Right and facing page top: The panoramic mountain views, dramatic architecture, and floor-to-ceiling vaulted windows make the Celebration Place one of our most popular spots for an indoor ceremony.

Facing page bottom: The Devotion Place's stone bridge, gazebo, and ponds inspire our guests year-round. Children love the outdoor wonderland, and brides and grooms love having such a variety of majestic backdrops to choose from.

Previous pages: Della Terra Mountain Chateau is all about seclusion and romance. The pristine night sky, undiluted by city lights, shows off the rich textures in the Continental Divide and surrounding Rocky Mountain landscape.

views

Having the support of the experts at your venue goes a long way when you're trying to realize your vision. When it comes to planning your wedding, there's no underestimating the value of someone who sees you for the unique couple you are.

ASPEN MEADOWS RESORT

DOUG CRAWFORD

Imagine a luxurious mountain town with amenities that are a perfect example of classic meets elegance, nature meets modernity. Then imagine a picturesque venue that embodies these qualities and defies expectation; that's how visitors and locals alike describe Aspen Meadows Resort.

Resting comfortably on 40 acres in Aspen's historic West End and home to the Aspen Institute, the resort boasts quite an interesting history that dates back to 1949. Inspired by European Bauhaus design, the resort is known for its art, architecture, and 360-degree views of the Rocky Mountains, not to mention indulgent accommodations.

However, Aspen Meadows really shines during events, which, considering the Aspen Institute's extensive history of hosting seminars, is no surprise. With three dining spaces—including Plato's, one of Aspen's premier fine dining establishments—two art galleries, more than 22,000 square feet of indoor event space, and numerous outdoor areas, the options can fulfill any style or type of event. From hosting various world leaders, including His Holiness the Dalai Lama, Biz Stone, former President Bill Clinton, and James Cameron, to large-scale lavish weddings and intimate dinners, the resort's portfolio not only impresses guests but speaks highly of the attention and care that the resort staff puts into each event.

The McNulty Ballroom is one of our most versatile spaces; it has such amazing light with the floor-to-ceiling windows and transom windows set within the high ceilings that the atmosphere is just exquisite.

Photograph courtesy of Aspen Meadows Resort

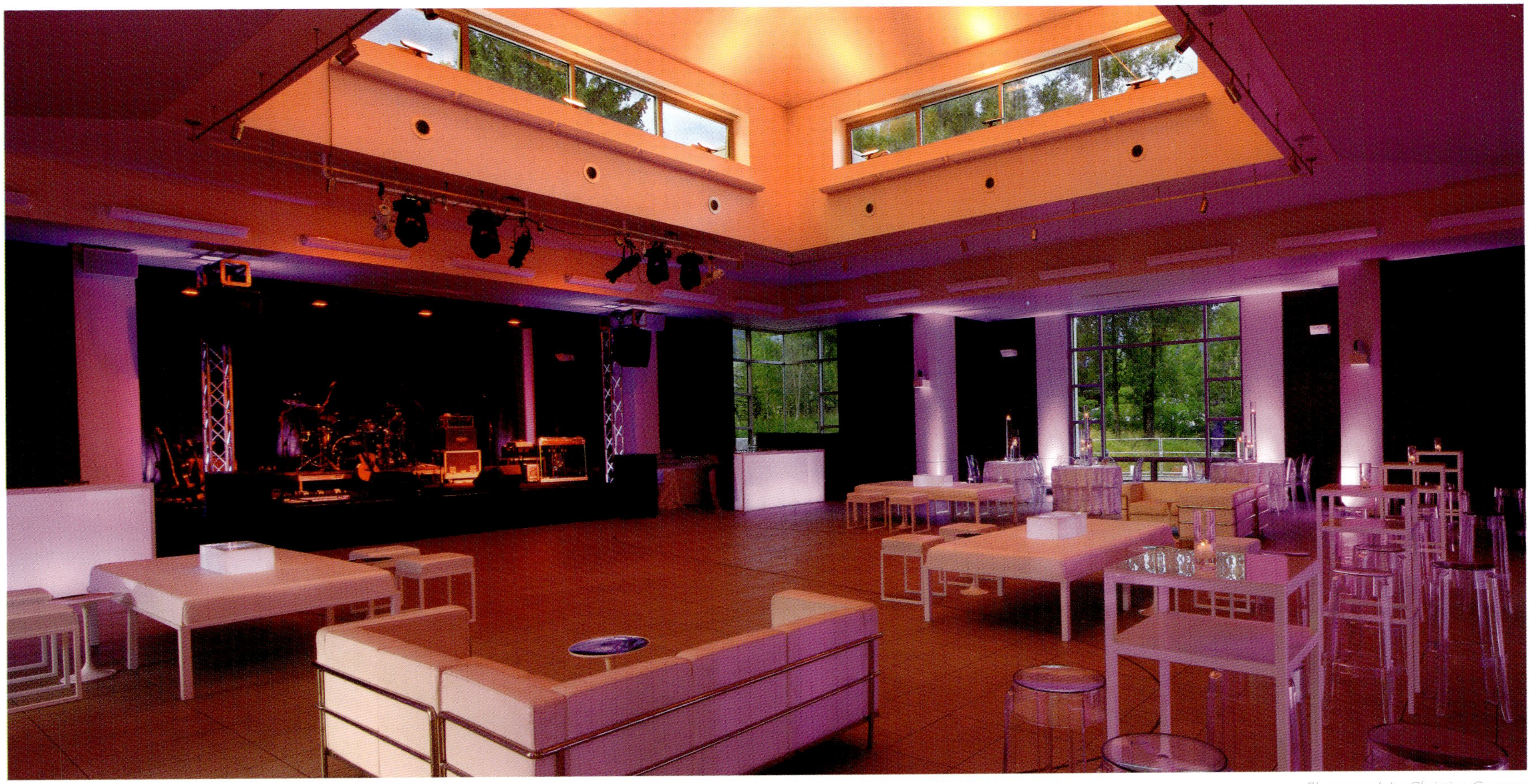

Photograph by Christina Capasso

Photograph by Christina Capasso

Photograph by Christina Capasso

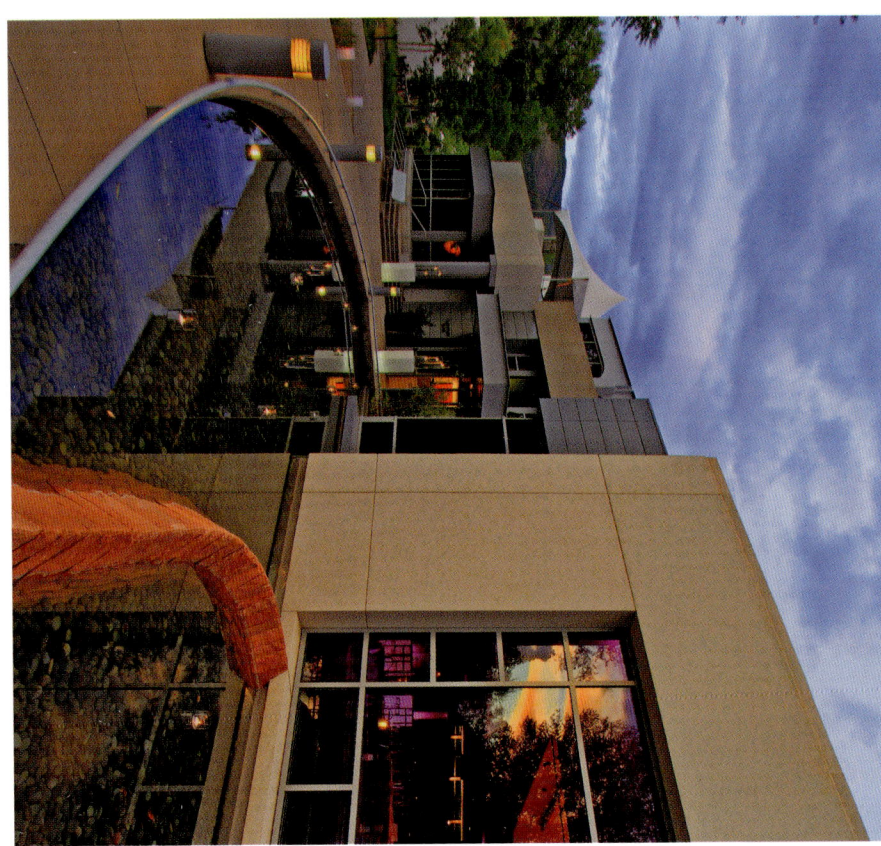

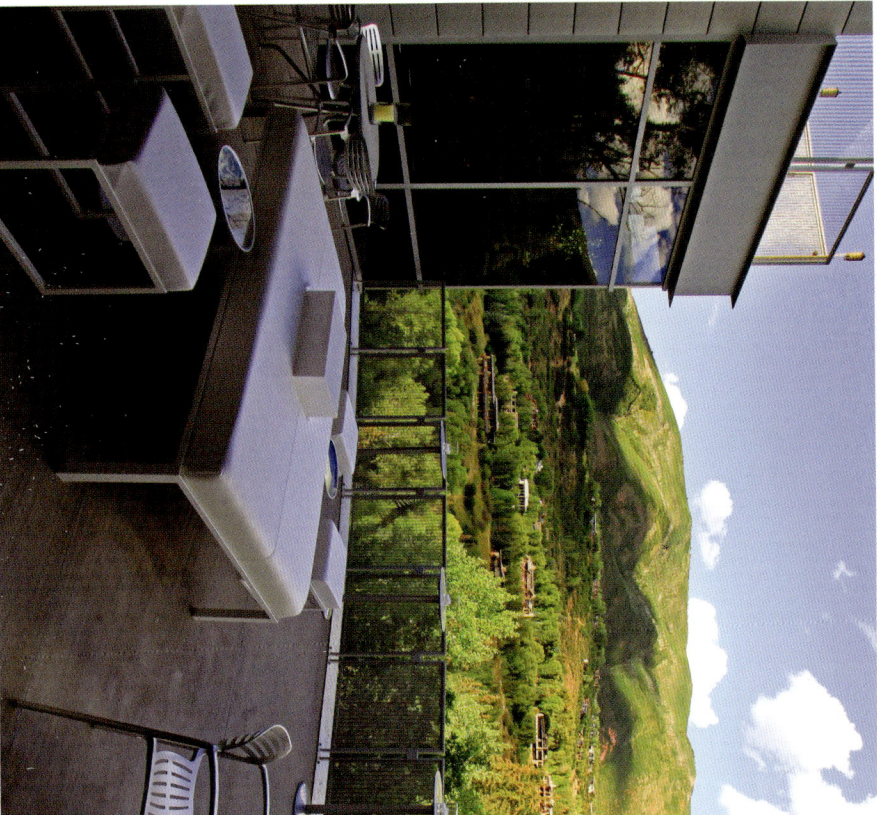

"Guests prefer venues that are unique, which is exactly why the Aspen Meadows has hosted so many events throughout its history."
—Doug Crawford

Right: A sea of Aspen trees and the breathtaking Rocky Mountains create what we think is a truly unique setting on the Merrill Patio, perfect for smaller, intimate gatherings.

Facing page top: The entire Doerr-Hosier building offers a variety of venues for our guests, including the airy McNulty Ballroom with a variety of outdoor terraces, not to mention a stunning backdrop.

Facing page bottom: The property was founded on the concept of uniting the mind, body, and spirit by tapping into the natural surroundings. Juxtaposing the views with clean architectural lines, the Doerr-Hosier Center emphasizes the beauty of both.

Photograph by Alice Koelle

views

Location is one of the most important aspects to any event. People are going to remember a unique location, not an enormous ballroom. The goal is to make it comfortable, a place where guests can enjoy company and the ambience. The key to selecting a successful space is to choose one that has a variety of places to explore outside of the main location.

JW Marriott Denver Cherry Creek

Artists are told to do what they do best, and as artists in entertainment, the staff at JW Marriott Denver Cherry Creek does just that. Partnering with the most elite event planners in the Denver area, the JW Marriott Denver Cherry Creek team makes it their top priority to focus on what is important as a venue: the guest experience. Nestled in the Cherry Creek neighborhood of Denver, it is the only hotel in the high-end shopping district, which includes boutiques, spas, and galleries. Still urban in location, the hotel boasts a mountainside feel and provides guests with the best of both worlds.

The event production team at JW Marriott Denver Cherry Creek works with party hosts every step of the way, extending a helping hand between the host and a stunning portfolio of partners perfectly suited to their celebration needs. With two versatile event spaces—the Grand Ballroom, a modern contemporary space for up to 200 people, and The Terrace at the JW Marriott Denver Cherry Creek, an outdoor space in the middle of urban Cherry Creek that can accommodate up to 150 people—it has become a popular event location for mitzvahs, sweet 16 parties, wedding receptions, and corporate events. The top priority of the event team at JW Marriott Denver Cherry Creek is to provide exceptional service to make every host's dream come true in an approachably elegant and unique venue.

The Terrace at JW Marriott Denver Cherry Creek, when enclosed—the perfect outdoor space in the middle of an urban neighborhood—is transformed into a mountain fall fantasy by Julie Gambrell of Classic Creations.

Photograph by Travis Broxton

Venue | 143

Photograph by Eric Stevenson

Photograph by CR Brinton

Photograph by Greg McBoat

Photograph by Travis Broxton

"Your venue should speak to your dreams the minute you walk through the door."
—Stephanie Geller

Right: A soft and romantic reception produced by Colorado Wedding Company, utilizing floral décor and draping by DesignWorks by Dave and Mike, and linen from Chair Covers and Linens, was held on the enclosed terrace. The terrace can be used as an indoor or outdoor event space, and some hosts choose to remove the temporary walls to open the party to the fresh Rocky Mountain air.

Facing page top left: The Grand Ballroom is the perfect setting for a bar mitzvah produced by Walli Richardson from Special Events Design and Calligraphy. The sports theme captures the focus of the entire room, which was draped for black light effect in order to feature the graffiti panels around the space. The artistry of Newberry Brothers comes to life in the centerpieces and Lendable Linens decorated the tables in Spandex.

Facing page top right: In a theme called Around the World, the Grand Ballroom provided Alisa Zaipler of Creative Events and Occasions with the opportunity to produce an elegant bat mitzvah featuring centerpieces by Newberry Brothers.

Facing page bottom left: The enclosed terrace became a winter fantasy for twin boy and girl's b'nai mitzvah in the hands of Amy Toltz-Miller. Newberry Brothers created the stunning centerpieces and guests settled into seating from Charming Chairs.

Facing page bottom right: A Japanese anime theme made the 16th birthday a hit when produced by JW Marriot Denver Cherry Creek in the enclosed terrace. Décor and linen were provided by DesignWorks by Dave and Mike.

views

When making the decision of where to host your event, following your intuition is extremely important. To make your event flawless and stress free, you need to establish trust in your vendors. Make sure that you connect with your event team to ensure that your vision becomes a blissful reality.

The Little Nell

When celebrities, high-end brands, and luxury sports car companies want to celebrate in Aspen, many flock to The Little Nell. Having served as the venue for Ferrari's Winter Driving Experience and as the launch party location for Veuve Clicquot in the Snow, The Little Nell transforms its party spaces into the vision of hosts' dreams. From coordinating large-scale wedding receptions to pampering guests' four-legged friends with personalized dog tags and epicurean treats, it is a venue where celebration is a daily occurrence.

Borrowing its name from the nearby mineshaft—which was named for claimant D. D. Fowler's paramour—The Little Nell is Aspen's legendary getaway destination and the only ski-in/ski-out hotel in the area. Established by the Aspen Skiing Company in 1989 as its flagship experience location, the resort provides guests with immediate access to all four local ski areas—Aspen Mountain, Aspen Highlands, Snowmass, and Buttermilk—and various après ski indulgences. Its location makes it a prime spot for visitors year-round. Guests of The Little Nell love to explore Aspen and get involved in local activities, including the artist and musical community; some even bring local musicians into their celebrations. Those who want to continue the revelry after an event may explore Aspen or partake of The Little Nell's array of culinary delights available at various onsite bars and restaurants.

Aspen isn't just for skiing. Poolside is a great place to lay back, relax, and enjoy the Colorado summer sky. Surrounding the pool is an array of pesticide-free edibles clipped for use in the resort's kitchens during the warmer months.

Photograph by Jason Dewey

Photograph by Alice Koelle

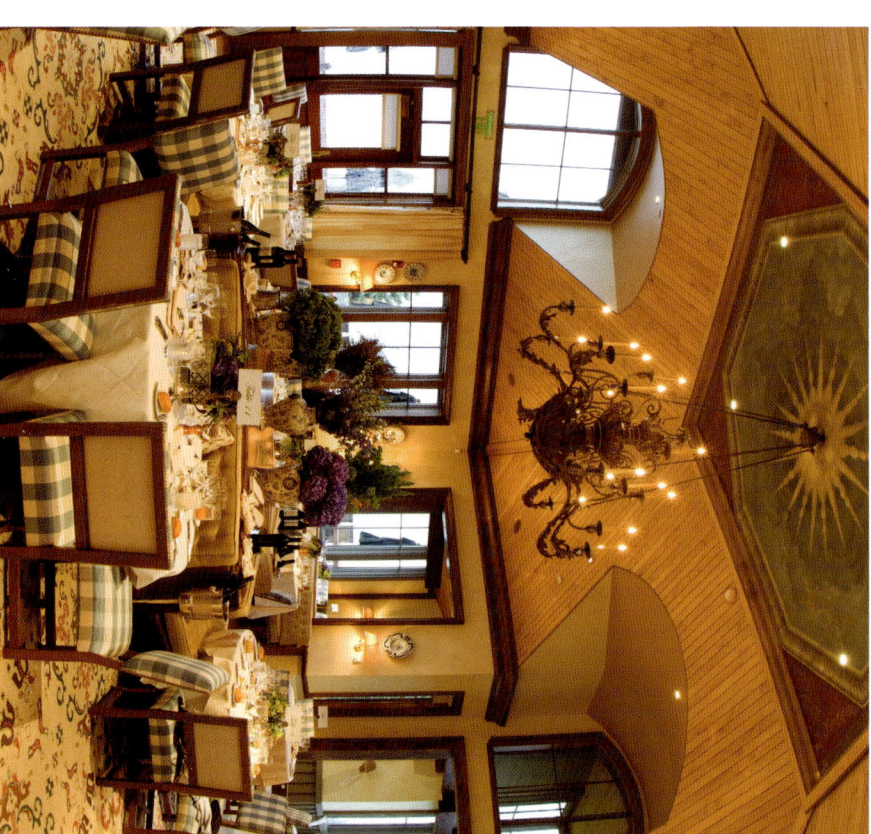

Photograph by Alice Koelle

Photograph by James Christianson

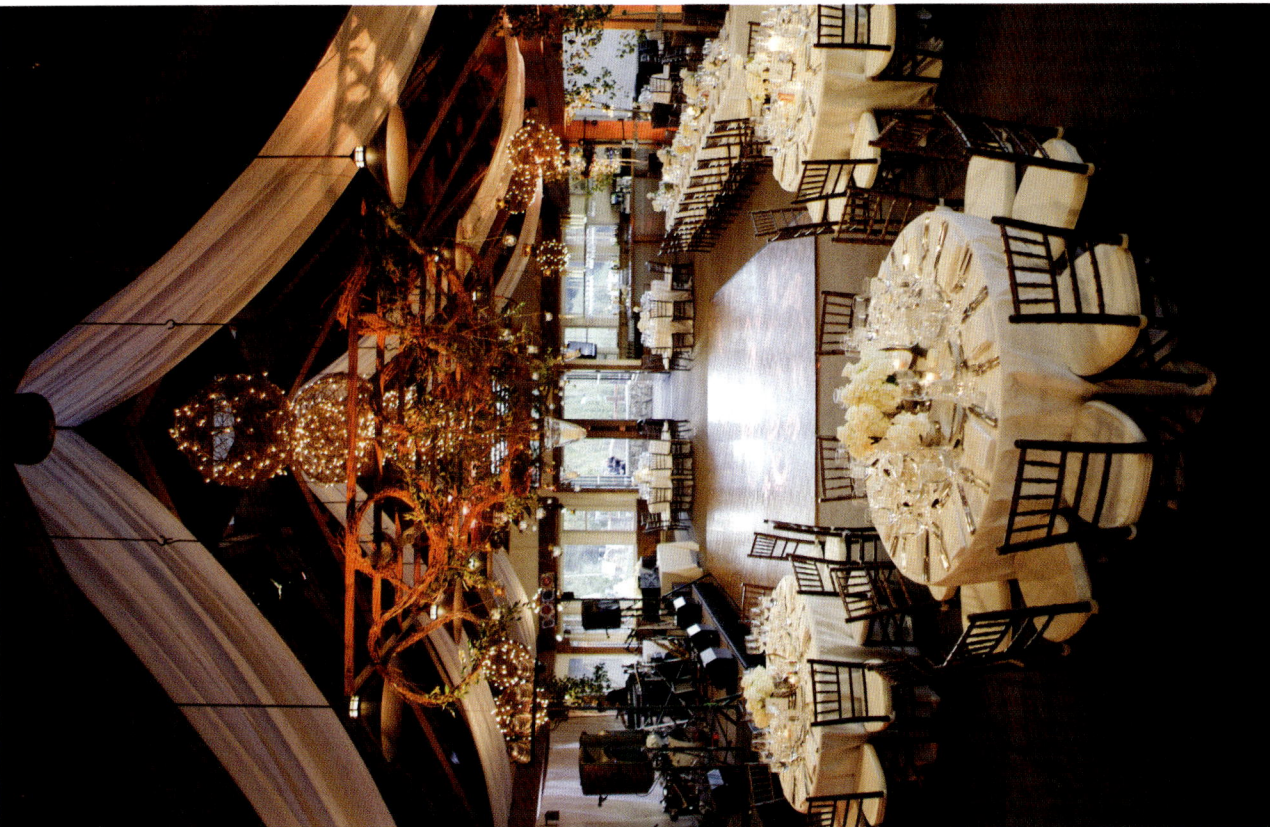

Photograph by James Christanson

"Look for a place that's legendary; a place people return to again and again."

—Sally Spaulding

Catering to a host's vision is what we do. We offer versatile spaces for parties, weddings, and corporate launches. From the sundeck, which allows guests a sweeping view of the Rockies, to the Aspen Mountain Club and the exclusive wedding deck situated atop the mountain, guests are treated to a unique experience with every visit. Our culinary staff—which includes a full-time butcher—sources ingredients from local providers and cures meats in-house, and our events team can turn the sundeck into a dream come true.

views

When planning an event, go with a venue that's well-established. You don't want to have to worry about everything coming together the right way, and selecting a location staffed with experienced experts means that even the smallest details are taken care of. Pick the venue based on the type of event you are planning and make sure the staff shares your party planning philosophy.

Palazzo Verdi

Sophistication meets elegance at Palazzo Verdi, a celebration venue located just south of Denver in Greenwood Village. Boasting an atmosphere that is innovative and stylish, Palazzo Verdi does double duty as part of the John Madden Company. Built in 2008, much of the LEED gold certified structure serves as office space during the work week. In the evenings and on weekends it transforms into an incredible event center, playing host to intimate rehearsal dinners, lavish weddings, elegant galas, custom business meetings, and celebration milestones.

With three main event spaces, including a museum on premises, the venue serves a variety of purposes. The Atrium at Palazzo Verdi, adorned with unique works of art by Colorado artists, is a dazzling space. At The MADDEN Museum of Art, visitors are treated to a rotating collection that spans 19th-century Italian paintings to present-day student works. The museum is the manifestation of John and Marjorie Madden's belief that art should be integrated into the community and business environment. Open to the public, the museum also functions as an event space for corporate galas and fundraising events. For more intimate gatherings, the European-style Mangia Bevi Café—complete with a stunning outdoor patio—and the Venetian Room serve small-scale private celebrations. With its emphasis on the arts and celebration, Palazzo Verdi is a diverse and dynamic space.

Palazzo Verdi is known for its artistic expression. Even from the outside, the building makes for a striking visual experience thanks to Lonnie Hanzon's *Chandelier Chardin*, a steel and glass wonder that descends 40 feet from the ceiling and features state-of-the-art lighting that changes colors and patterns.

Photograph by WonderWorks Studios

Photograph by Trystan Photography

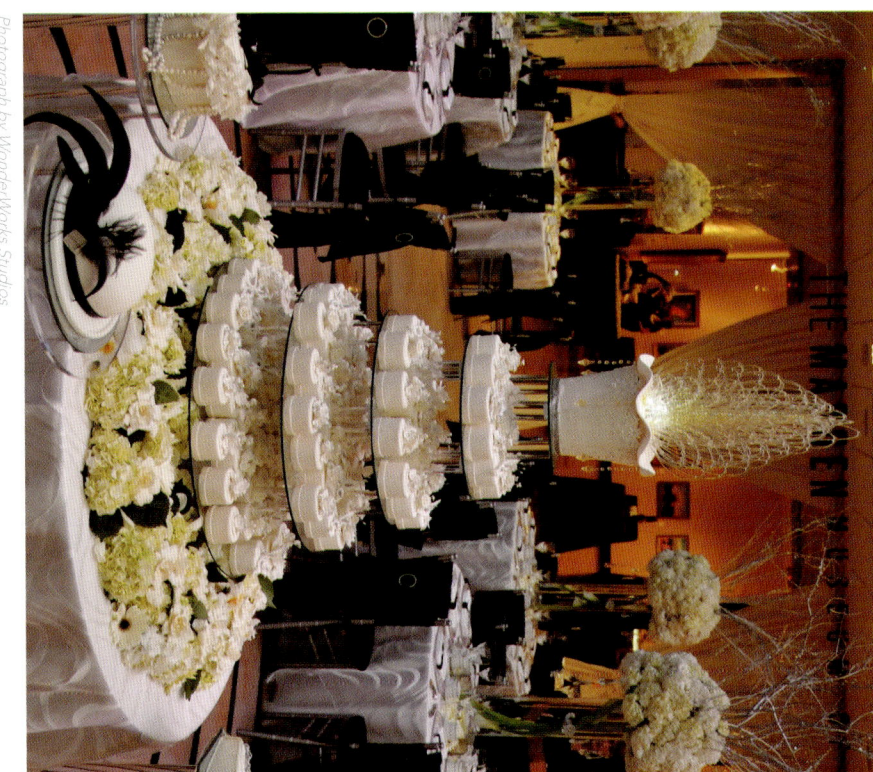

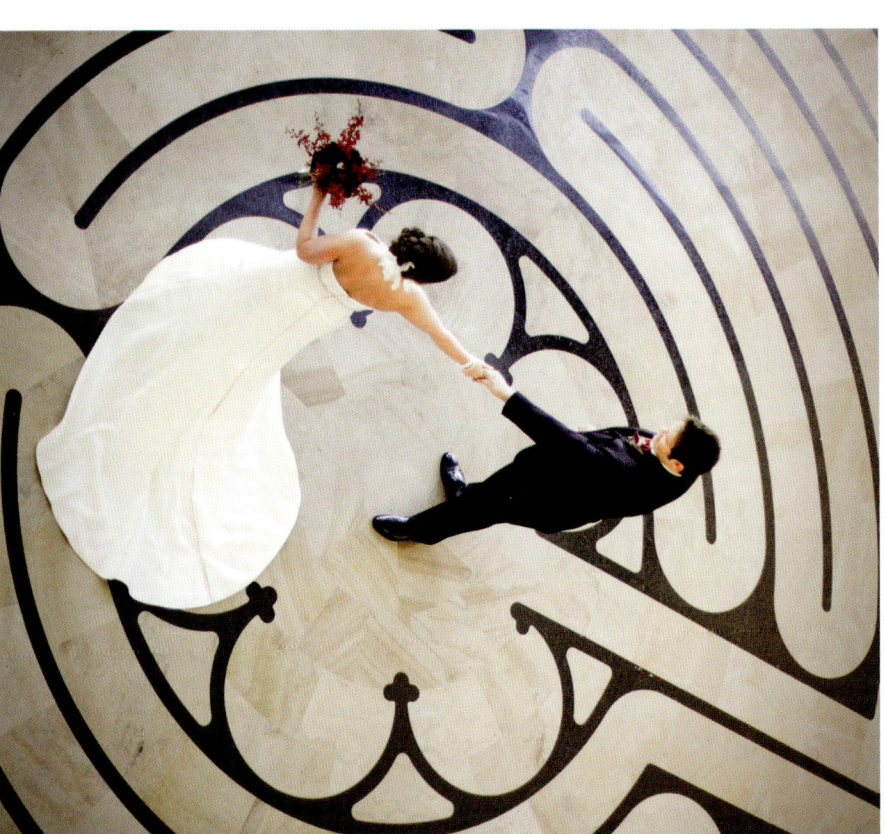

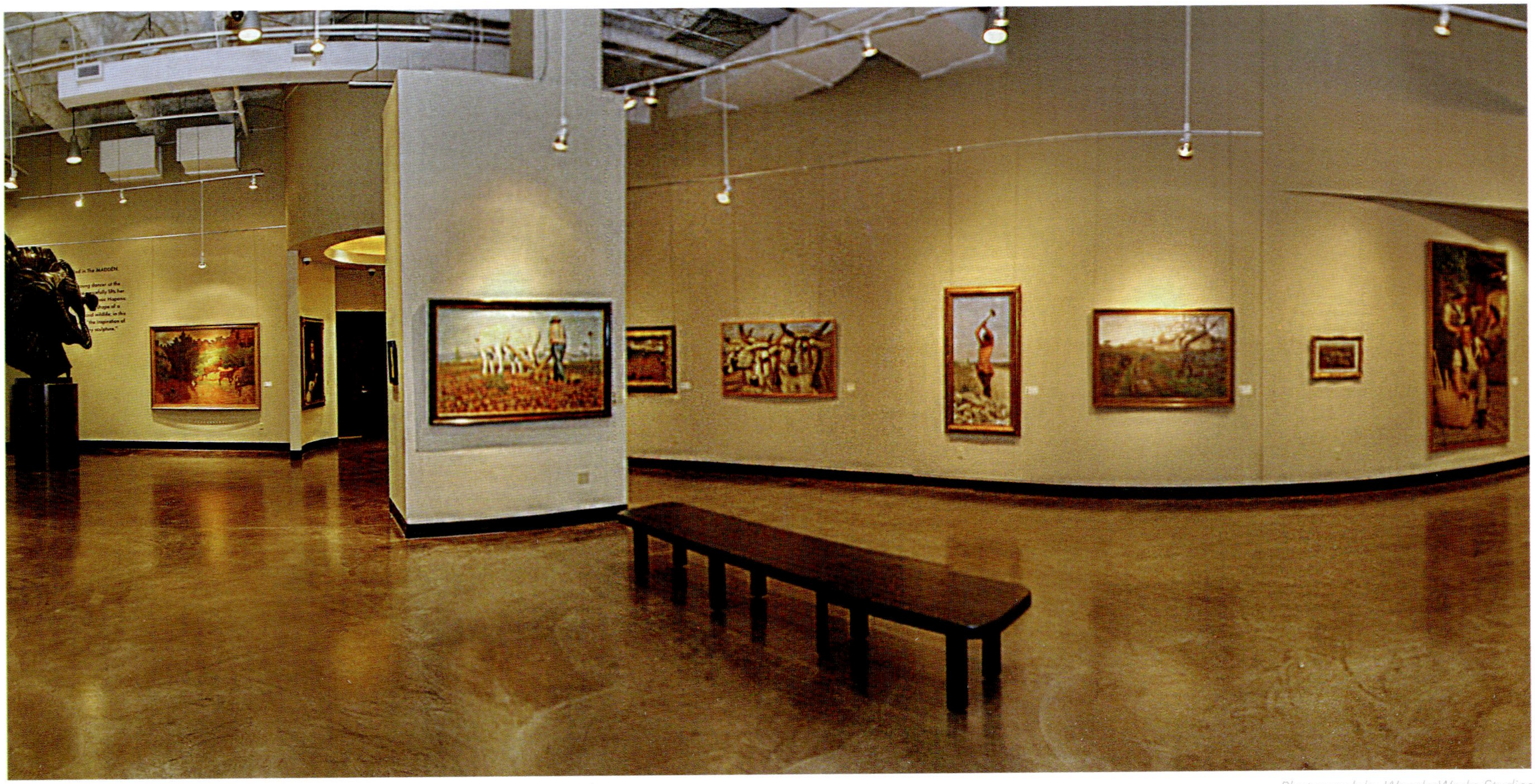

Photograph by WonderWorks Studios

"Every event is unique; it should first and foremost reflect the host's personality."
—Leslee Russell

Right: Below Hanzon's chandelier is *Chartes Labyrinth* by Roger Leitner. The 42-foot-wide installation is a recreation of a 13th-century French maze, composed of stone and pieced together just so to eliminate the use of grout; it takes 34 turns just to reach the center.

Facing page: The presence of art and culture adds an extra layer to the celebration of milestone events. When you're surrounded by beauty in different forms, it heightens the drama.

views

Your venue should capture your heart. It should be beautiful and elegant, and just as unique as you are.

SEAWELL GRAND BALLROOM

Shakespearian-themed nuptials, floating DJs, aerial dancers, multimedia spectacles—no vision is too extravagant and no idea too fanciful at the Seawell Grand Ballroom. Centrally located in the heart of Denver's Theatre District, the Seawell Grand Ballroom was built to host extraordinary events, and since 1998 the venue's innovative staff has been individually designing and seamlessly executing unforgettable affairs in the 10,000-square-foot space.

The monochromatic base color scheme, state-of-the-art audiovisual and lighting systems, and scalability provide the requisite canvas for creating a full spectrum of dramatic, inspiring events, from grandiose to intimate and bold to simply elegant. Marry this with panoramic views of the lower downtown skyline and the stunning Rocky Mountains, and you've got the perfect stage for life's important milestones, dynamic corporate celebrations, and fundraising galas.

Finding inspiration in their theatrical roots, and the intrinsic creative license that begets, professional onsite designers, coordinators, and technical staff work collaboratively to refine a host's vision and bring it to life in a memorable and personal way. Drawing on a combined 50 years of theatrical and technical experience, the in-house team is able to customize design, lighting, sound, and video to add drama and set the tone, while planners ensure each detail is vetted and everyone hits their mark. At the Seawell, it is about ushering dreams into reality and composing indelible, distinctive celebrations.

As a full event production venue, we manage the process from beginning to end. Whether working with the in-house team or outside vendors, the end result is always a vibrant, sophisticated, exclusive event that is meticulously crafted and flawlessly implemented.

Photograph by Jenna Walker Photographers

Photograph by Studio JK Photography

Photograph by Lynda Hanshaw

Photograph by broxtonArt

Photograph by DEVO Photography

"Every event we produce is designed and built from the ground up."
—Dawn Williams

Right: A favorite of our newly wedded couples is a quintessential shot of their names emblazoned on the ballroom's theatrically-styled marquee.

Facing Page: The ballroom features a multitude of rigging and lighting opportunities. The wave form ceiling in and of itself is magnificent—as daylight wanes, thousands of fiber optic lights create a star-filled canopy overhead. Augment this with vivid lighting, artfully hung draperies, and personalized décor, and it is possible to produce any mood or feeling from sultry speakeasy to elegant gala and everything in between.

views

Setting clear goals and expectations is a critical first step in planning. Know your priorities and establish a realistic budget, then use this as a foundation for brainstorming ideas.

Ambience

DesignWorks by Dave and Mike

DAVID SQUIRES | MICHAEL ROFFINO

Open the senses and inspiration will be found everywhere, from nature's incredible color palette to the linear purpose of synthetic form. That's the philosophy applied to all aspects of event design and production at DesignWorks by Dave and Mike—and just one of many reasons why expectations are surpassed every time the team is involved with an event.

As a multifaceted firm with nearly 50 employees well versed in design, florals, graphics, printing, carpentry, and textiles, DesignWorks' extensive portfolio is quite impressive. From delicate pink rhinestone napkin embellishments of a baby shower to the grand floral arches of a wedding ceremony to multiday sales conferences with décor that encourages guests to strive for their best, every event captures the senses through innovative, fresh design.

DesignWorks is led by president and florist extraordinaire David Squires and CEO and design aficionado Michael Roffino, offering 40-plus years of combined experience. David, who is always in perpetual motion, brings incredible floral talent and design know-how, relying on his experience with his popular floral and home accessory shop. Michael, who has a background in fine art and interior design, injects high energy throughout the firm and approaches design with architectural sensibilities. Since DesignWorks' founding in 2000, they have inspired a team that has designed and produced presidential, celebrity, and elite social events around the world that invoke jubilation at every turn.

Creating an intimate space within the 30-foot-tall, dome-shaped room at The Aspen Institute was a challenge. A complete transformation of the room resulted in a vintage European holiday look. We topped it off with a beautiful chandelier, which established an inviting, unified atmosphere for the New Year's Eve event.

Photograph by Alice Koelle Photography

Design, Floral & Production | 161

Photograph by Mike Roffino, DesignWorks

"Inspiration comes to me through texture, pattern, and the drama each individual flower provides."
—David Squires

Photograph by Mike Roffino, DesignWorks

For a contemporary and sophisticated wedding reception at the Seawell Grand Ballroom in The Denver Center for the Performing Arts, we found inspiration in the venue's lobby, which features a circular motif. The crowning glory was the 10-foot-wide-diameter chandeliers that effervesced with sophisticat on and a hip sparkle. Centerpieces accented with stylized bands of button mums reinforced the spherical design while adding texture and a modern elegance to the event.

"Every day for me is like a fine art class. I get to work with my colored pencils, T-square, and color palette to breathe life into new designs."
—Michael Roffino

Photograph by Jared Wilson Photography

Above: All-white aisle arrangements in clear, elevated cylinders were our choice for a clean, contemporary look at the Hyatt Regency Denver. Because of the venue's natural brown tones, we utilized a soft ceiling drape to enhance the romantic ambience while also directing guests' eyes toward the huppah.

Facing page top: The use of floral elements can vary widely from one event to another; acrylic candelabras at one event evoked the illusion of a floating arrangement, while the dramatic tree structures and hanging crystals created a whimsical forest inspired by a treasured childhood book of the bride's.

Facing page bottom: We always do our best to accommodate any requests or traditions that express the hosts' personality or goals. For an elegant wedding at The Broadmoor in Colorado Springs, the family asked us to avoid any sticks that protruded in opposing directions because those represented infertility. The intimate ceremony space was the starting point for the unique, awe-inspiring atmosphere.

Photograph by Nathan Welton, Dreamtime Images

Photograph by Mike Rafino, DesignWorks

Photograph by Eric Stephenson Photography

Photograph by Mike Rafino, DesignWorks

Design, Floral & Production | 165

"Intimate weddings are all about personalization and the opportunity to focus on humble details creating sentimental value."
—Michael Roffino

Left and facing page top: To appease both the young, gothic couple who preferred an edgy design, and the traditional parents, we created a ceremony setting at The Stanley Hotel in Estes Park that incorporated classic white florals with an artistic damask pattern in the runner. The elegant, gothic reception required a floor-to-ceiling transformation, including building columns to support the ceiling canopy.

Facing page bottom: Originally a boardroom with white walls, the space within the Denver Art Museum took shape only after intense research on King Tutankhamun's tomb. Every element, from the hieroglyphic wall to the variety of fruit, was designed with such accuracy that even Dr. Zahi Hawass, the secretary general of the Supreme Council of Antiquities in Egypt, said the elements were historically appropriate.

Art of Celebration | 168

Photograph by Stevie Crecelius, WonderWorks Studios

Photograph by Stevie Crecelius, WonderWorks Studios

Photograph by Stevie Crecelius, WonderWorks Studios

Above: Even for events with no specific theme, design plays a major role. The dimensional, 20-foot-tall structures created a dramatic focal point and reinforced curves in the company's logo at the Hyatt Regency Denver Tech Center.

Facing page top: The scale within a room is always a main concern. Within the Fillmore Auditorium in Denver, we added 14-foot-high centerpieces supporting televisions broadcasting the events on stage and electrifying colorful effects for an MTV-inspired mitzvah.

Facing page bottom: Inspired by upscale Victorian and garden labyrinth concepts, we provided stark contrast in the Seawell Grand Ballroom with black and white tones and large, banquet-style tables. The challenge was to outdo the previous year's holiday event without blowing the company's budget.

"Don't narrow your vision or you may miss something that could provide wonderful inspiration."
—Michael Roffino

Photograph by Lynda Hanshaw Photography

"The elated look on the host's face when he or she walks into the event space is invaluable to us; we wouldn't trade that for anything."
—David Squires

At the JW Marriott Denver Cherry Creek, a sophisticated luncheon celebrating the arrival of a baby girl featured pink tones and whimsical carousels. Poles, inspired by carousels, connected each table together with gorgeous fabric draped along the ceiling. We took common children's toys and gave them sophistication, like the alphabet blocks used as coffee and side tables where guests could gather.

views

Key elements for successful event design include sculpting the room, bringing elements off the floor and dropping them from the ceiling, and engulfing guests in an environment that engages all of their senses.

Newberry Brothers

PAULA NEWBERRY-ARNOLD | KIEN ARNOLD

When people bandy about the term "family business," chances are they are imagining a multi-generational, extended-family, household-name empire like the one started by Weldon Newberry and his two brothers right after WWII. They specialized in the wholesale market, establishing greenhouses, and growing their trademark Colorado Carnation, the first trademarked flower in the US. In later years, Weldon's wife, Elizabeth, launched the floral side of the company, eventually sharing ownership of the company with her daughter, Paula Newberry-Arnold, until Elizabeth's passing in 2011. Paula is now the current mastermind behind the Newberry brand.

Aided by a skilled team of artisans, the Newberry reputation rests on each team member's ability to express both passion and patience while giving hosts the most bang for their buck. They start out by gathering the details of the bride's or birthday honoree's wish list and vision for the event. Then, magically, they find a way to fit all of their requests into the budget. No project is too large or too small, and since Paula owns the greenhouses, brides who just need a few flowers and plants for a DIY wedding are greeted as warmly as those staging elaborate celebrations.

Paula and her team are pros when it comes to dealing with the unexpected, like the time on top of Vail Mountain when the tear-down team experienced a power outage and had to disassemble an entire wedding site by the headlights of a van while being pestered by a large, angry porcupine. Of course the team took it in stride, the bride never knew a thing, and the team was back at work the next morning, ready for the next challenge.

The Four Seasons asked us to create a dream centerpiece to be used in its new promotional materials. To design an exquisite wedding centerpiece, we took our cues from the gown, the ballroom, and the exquisite linens that had been brought in for the photo shoot. Because the room is an extraordinary space with contemporary crystal chandeliers, we wanted to create a floral piece that brides would not only respond to, but that they could actually envision having at their own wedding.

Floral Design | 173

Photograph by Studio JK Photography

"Planning a wedding is easy. Step one: choose your venue. Step two: choose your dress. Step three: choose your bridesmaids' dresses. Step four: call your florist."
—Paula Newberry-Arnold

Right: For a wedding reception at the Seawell Grand Ballroom, we worked with the mother-of-the-groom Cindy Farber to create an assemblage of abstract topiaries using white hydrangea and roses. We then added five-foot crystal candelabras with spherical drops of flowers and a wall of handmade, 20-inch paper flowers. The effect was remarkable.

Facing page top: Krystal Shanahan's July 4th wedding was a dream in blue and white accented by a lot of candlelight. We chose a flower palette of blue delphinium, blue hydrangea, and white phalaenopsis orchids for the ceremony and the reception, and topped the chair backs with white phalaenopsis orchid blooms.

Facing page bottom: Sometimes you don't need flowers at all. Case in point: a black-light bar mitzvah with a graffiti theme and a neon color scheme inspired by a Coldplay video. Golf, skiing, football, and hockey silhouettes served as centerpieces and chair backs were wrapped in neon green, blue, and orange fabric.

Photograph by Frances Photography

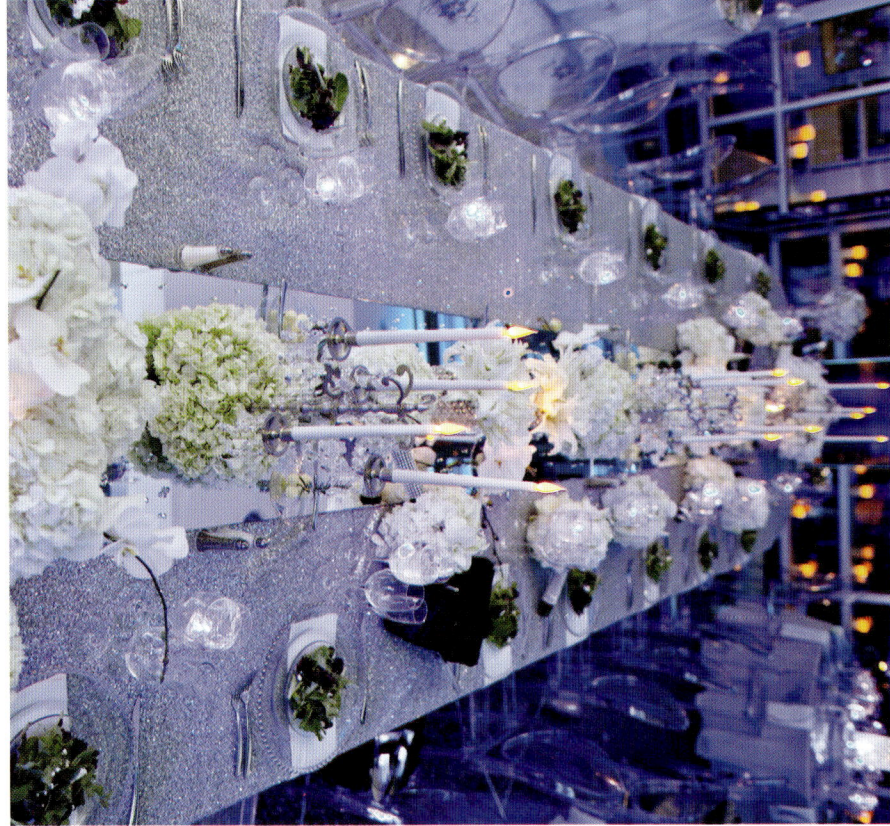

"Online idea boards and tablet computers are the greatest thing to happen to event planning since email."

—Paula Newberry-Arnold

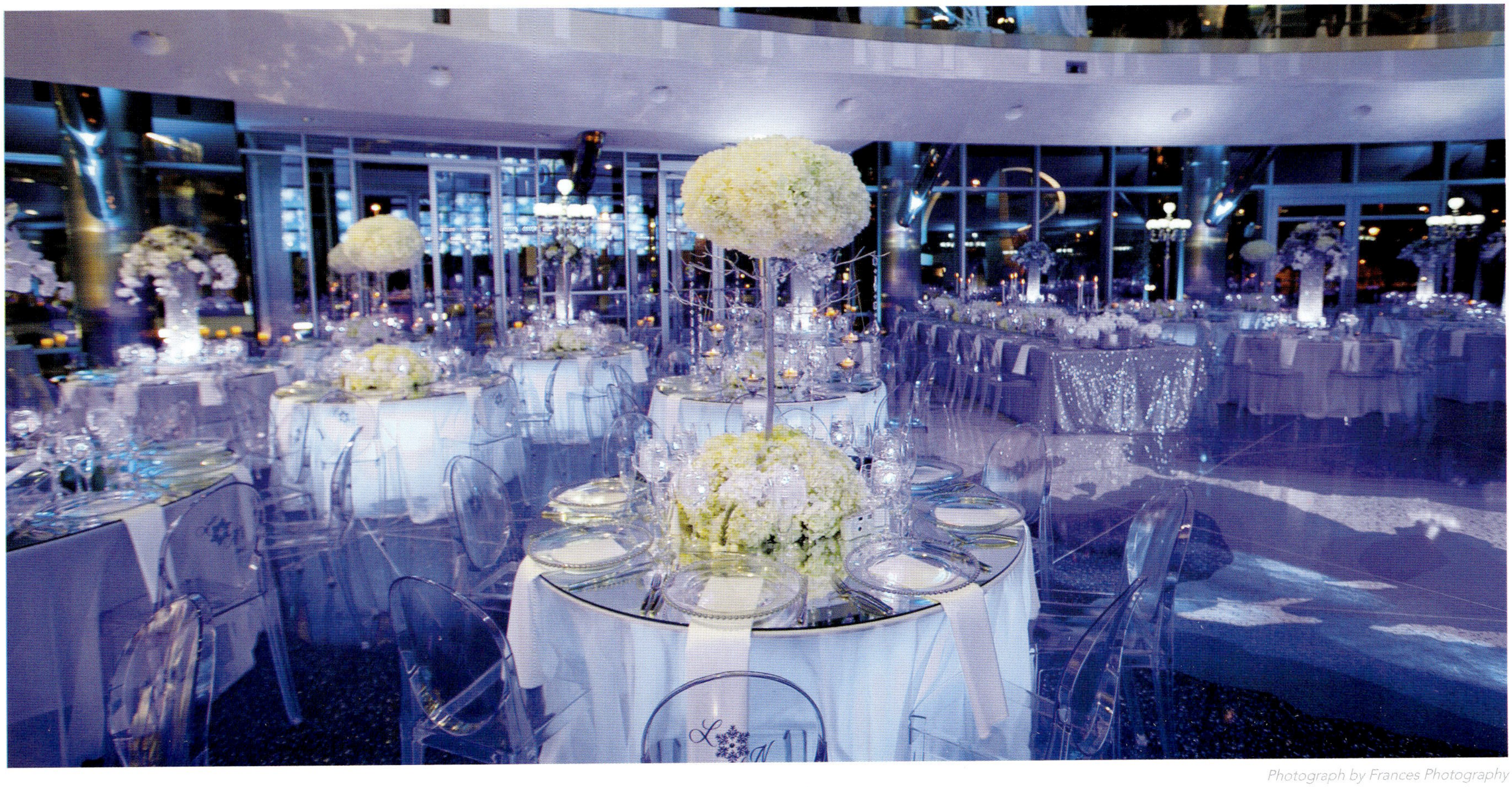

Photograph by Frances Photography

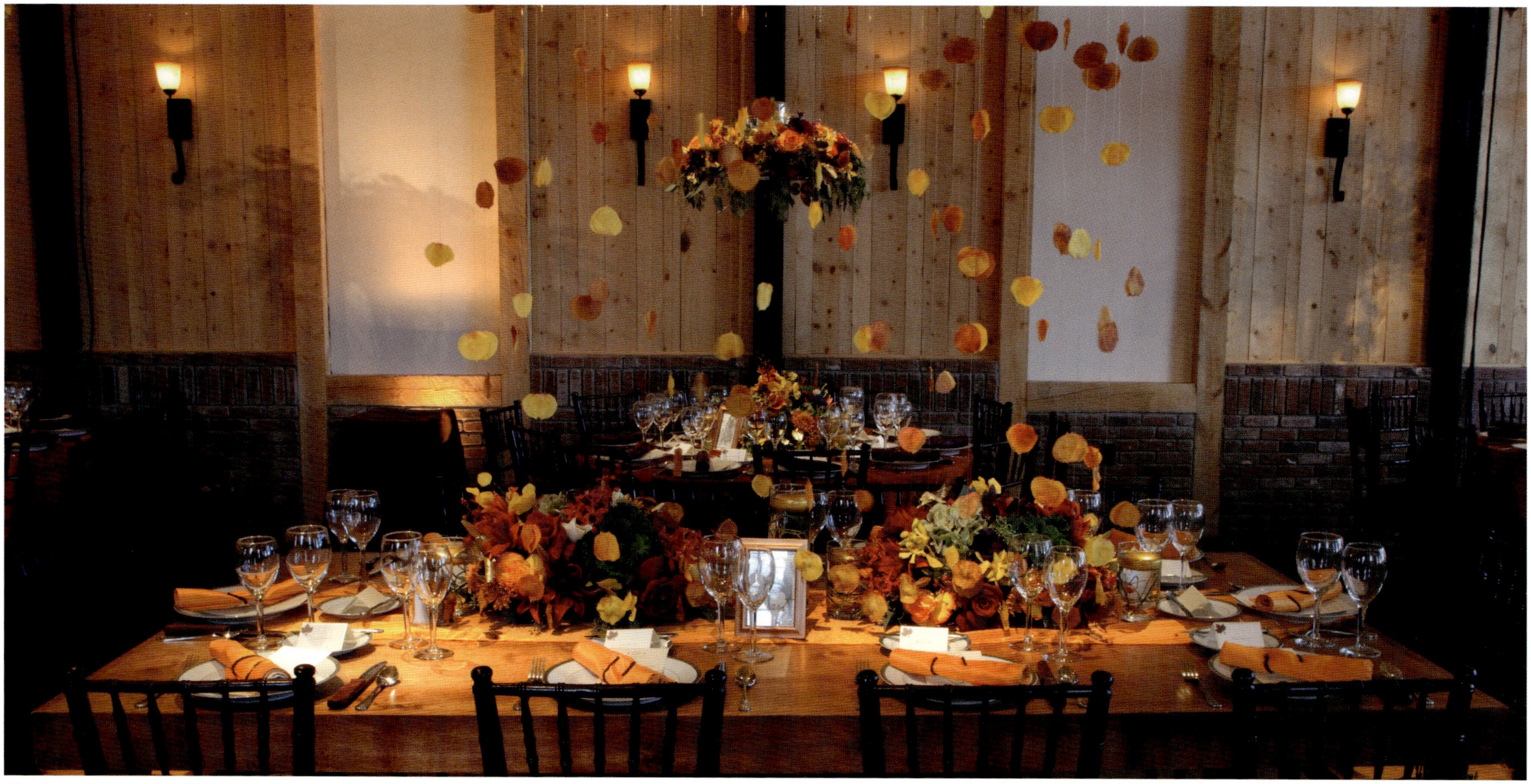

Photograph by Moments of Expression Photography

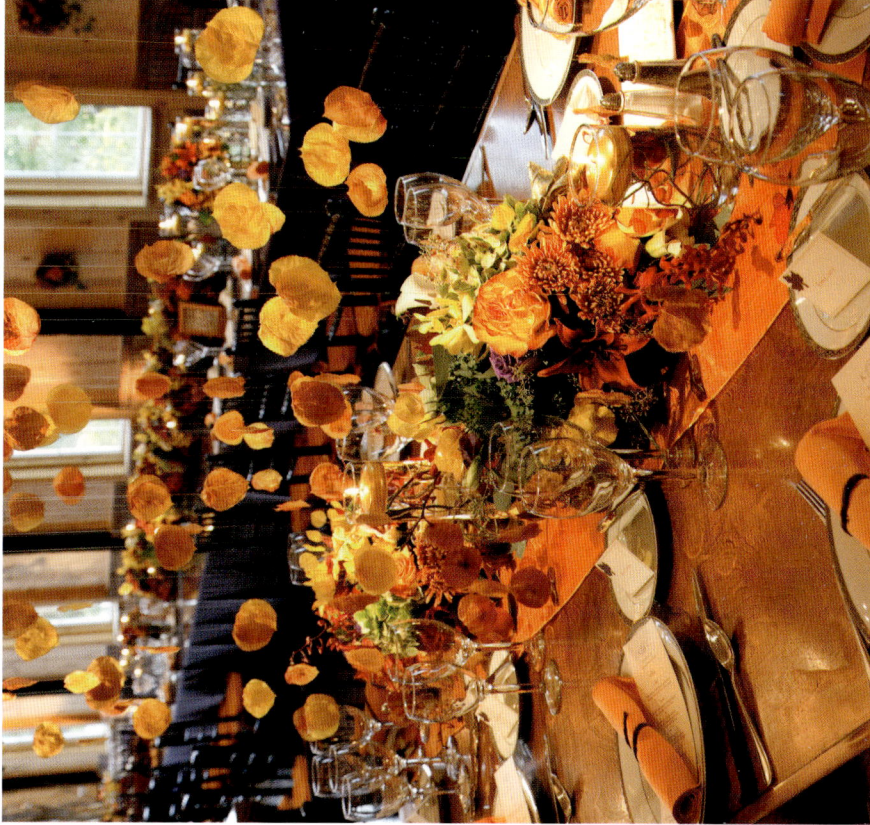

Above and right: Seasonal weddings are beautiful. When a bride wanted a fall theme with an elegant twist, we strung faux aspen leaves on fishing line to create a falling-leaves theme above the tables. Even though the venue was a horse farm, the effect was stylish yet rustic. For centerpieces we used lanterns, LED pillar candles, and a jumble of mini calla lilies, hydrangea, roses, ranunculus, lisianthus, and orchids.

Facing page: A New Year's Eve wedding at The Cable Center at the University of Denver got an extra dose of bling with Lucite ghost chairs from Charming Chairs, emblazoned with a snowflake and rhinestone decal in honor of the bride's new name, which happened to be Snow. We made some centerpieces from crystal candelabras, some from hydrangea trees with hanging crystals, and others from crystal containers belonging to the bride.

Photograph by Moments of Expression Photography

Photograph by Jared Wilson Photography

"Wedding planning is the tangible expression of shared hope."
—Paula Newberry-Arnold

Right: When a bride and groom have differing styles, sometimes the best thing to do is divide and conquer. While the bride had full reign over the ceremony, the groom designed the reception to replicate a nightclub. Centerpieces were lighted from above and tables from below with color-changing LED lighting. Phalaenopsis orchids hung over the top of centerpieces created from repurposed wire-webbed lampshades.

Facing page top: When a couple whose wedding we had designed a decade ago in Denver was ready to hold their 10-year vow renewal in Las Vegas, we were more than happy to contribute. We worked with the coordinator for both the past and present celebrations, and were able to create completely one-of-a-kind décor. For centerpieces on the leaf-shaped tables, we created an effect where roses, orchids, green cabbage roses, and hydrangea appeared to be spilling out of toppled crystal containers.

Facing page bottom left: When a bride loves pink, we give it to her. The bride wanted a color scheme that ranged from light pink to traditional pink with light green accents and crystal embellishments. We covered the vases with crystal strands, tied them off with a band of flowers, and let crystal strands drape down into the arrangement on the table. We accented the Lucite Chiavari chairs with hydrangea and placed green hydrangea on the napkins. The room was a sea of antique green hydrangea, traditional pink roses, pink branch roses, and ivy.

Facing page bottom right: Expect very different results when a bride designs the ceremony and the groom has free rein over the reception. For the ceremony at the Four Seasons Hotel Denver, we laid down a glamorous acrylic aisle runner and used the hotel's own exquisite chandeliers as the crown of the huppah. The legs of the huppah were hanging crystal strands, and a backdrop was created by combining fabric with more hanging crystals. As a surprise for the bride, the groom arranged to have a hedge of pink and white flowers lining the aisle for her arrival.

views

Help us help you: Arrive with a direction, some favorite looks, and a list of favorite flowers. Give your designer a sense of your budget so they can keep money in mind when they are designing.

THE ASPEN BRANCH

BETH GILL

If an empty room is a blank canvas, then Beth Gill's chosen artistic tools come in the form of breathtaking floral arrangements, linens, and event décor. As the owner of The Aspen Branch studio, Beth uses her creative energy to exceed expectations, utilizing her acute sense of ever-evolving trends and styles.

It is immediately obvious that The Aspen Branch team loves what they do. The amount of care and attention they devote to every event stands as a testament to their passion; flowers are more than just pretty pieces of décor. When an eye-catching floral centerpiece is placed in the middle of a table, it draws the eyes of the seated guests to the center and thus to each other. In the midst of admiring a stunning arrangement, strangers are compelled to trade glances and conversation. Beautiful centerpieces bring a table together both decoratively and socially, and set the mood for the memories about to be created.

Our winter wonderland wedding challenge was to create an outdoor Rocky Mountain feel in an area that protected the guests from the chilly elements. A clear-top tent was placed in the courtyard of the St. Regis Aspen Resort. Light fabric swags allowed a great view of the sky while the suspended huppah made from magnolias, hydrangea, and roses added elegance with a modern twist.

Photograph by Alice Koelle

When working within a rustic atmosphere, contemporary touches keep the soirée from looking cliché. Asian lanterns hung from the ceiling, iron lanterns hung from wagon wheels, trays of candles, and arrangements of local flowers are wonderful elements. Adding mirrors and fabric to the room creates interest and softens the space.

"Candlelight creates magic."
—Beth Gill

Photograph by Thisbe Grace

"Flowers bring life to an event with colors and shapes only nature can create."

—Beth Gill

Flowers amplify the romance of a celebration. Adding charming elements like antique glass for a centerpiece or vintage broaches to bouquets makes for nostalgic and elegant arrangements. In addition to flowers, well-chosen vases, candlesticks, and fabric elevate interest and make the space the host's own for the day.

views

The ideal floral and event designer will go out on a limb for you—seasons or location shouldn't be an automatic reason for rejecting an idea. Look for someone willing to take risks and bend the rules to make your ideal celebration a reality.

Bethel Party Rentals

MARTIN HERRERA | MARIA HERRERA

It takes a special kind of person to see losing their job as a message from on high, but when Martin Herrera found himself without gainful employment after seven years of working with a Carbondale party rental company, he took it as a sign that God wanted him to start his own business. What started as a sign became a lesson in perseverance. In 2005, Martin hung out his party rentals shingle and were soon booking large weddings as far away as Durango, Summit County, Telluride, and Utah.

As the business grew, a modest storage facility would no longer suffice. There were platforms to store, machines to maintain, and fabrics to preserve. These days, it takes a 12,000-square-foot storage space to hold the full spectrum of tents, linens, chairs, flatware, and accoutrements the Herreras have amassed to create and populate their customized, luxury event tents. Credit their success to a combination of employees who believe in taking care of the customers like family, an insistence on tip-top quality in all of their materials, and a faith that every member of the company has the wherewithal to bring even the most complicated requests to life.

Challenge fuels this family business—Martin's wife, sons, daughters, and sons-in-law each have his or her role—especially during 11th-hour surprises, like when a bride decides she wants a larger tent five hours before the wedding is set to begin. Of course they make it work—that's the beauty of divine intervention. And after a decade of smiling faces, it's clear to everyone that Martin and his family have found their true calling.

We love putting together outdoor events in Aspen because the Roaring Fork Valley and Mount Sopris provide such a variety of storybook backdrops. Brides love our 60-by-80-foot Losberger tent; it's large enough for a huge extended family and the French windows are perfect for framing those award-winning views. And with Colorado's rapidly changing weather, having the option for open or closed sides provides ultimate peace of mind.

Photograph by Susana Anchondo

views

"It's important to think creatively, especially in Colorado, where the mountain locations and rocky terrain provide endless site challenges."
—Maria Herrera

Many people don't realize how luxurious tents can be. We go to great lengths to make our tents feel as opulent and as much like a permanent structure as possible. Swagging the interior and ceiling in gorgeous fabric makes the space feel more like a cathedral than a temporary structure. Add chandeliers, living topiaries, and lounge areas, and suddenly the guests feel like they've entered a private club. Swap in a tent with a transparent ceiling and all of that beautiful high-elevation sunshine provides the most flattering lighting you could ask for.

Your events should reflect your dreams. Work with a provider who is not only willing to engage with your fantasy, but who also has the tools and imagination to bring it to life.

LINENS UNLIMITED

LINDA BLUHM

Linda Bluhm, owner of Linens Unlimited, takes a great deal of pride in living up to the company's name, providing an unlimited linen selection for every special occasion. As purveyors of specialty rental linens and accessories, Linda and her staff make sure the world of linen is at their fingertips. Linda has focused on creating relationships with just about every linen manufacturer, both nationally and internationally, so that she and her team can offer event hosts an enormous selection in all budgets.

For hosts, that means one-stop shopping at its finest. Fabulous fabrics, countless colors, and nature-inspired textures are readily available. The stress of shopping endlessly online is completely removed so that planning becomes an exciting adventure of crafting and executing the vision. It means hosts can actually look forward to the process, whether the event is intimate or grand, casual or formal.

With more than a decade in the industry, Linda's attention to detail and eye for perfection are undeniable. Each event has to meet the highest of standards. Every linen detail is checked and, if needed, redone before her team leaves the venue. That's the kind of dedication that makes events successful.

Linens Unlimited provides full, personalized service to every host. Whether it's pressing linens onsite, creating a unique napkin fold or chair tie, providing custom items, or using fabrics in unusual ways, the team accepts the challenge. Linda considers every host as unique and special as the linens she provides, and the team at Linens Unlimited works hard to turn each event vision into a stunning reality.

We wanted the linens to complement the sparkle of the Four Seasons Hotel Denver's dramatic chandeliers while providing a softer background for the dinnerware and florals. Gold mesh under an ivory chiffon parachute provides a beautiful touch of elegance, while the short bustle and train on the chair covers hints of a wedding gown.

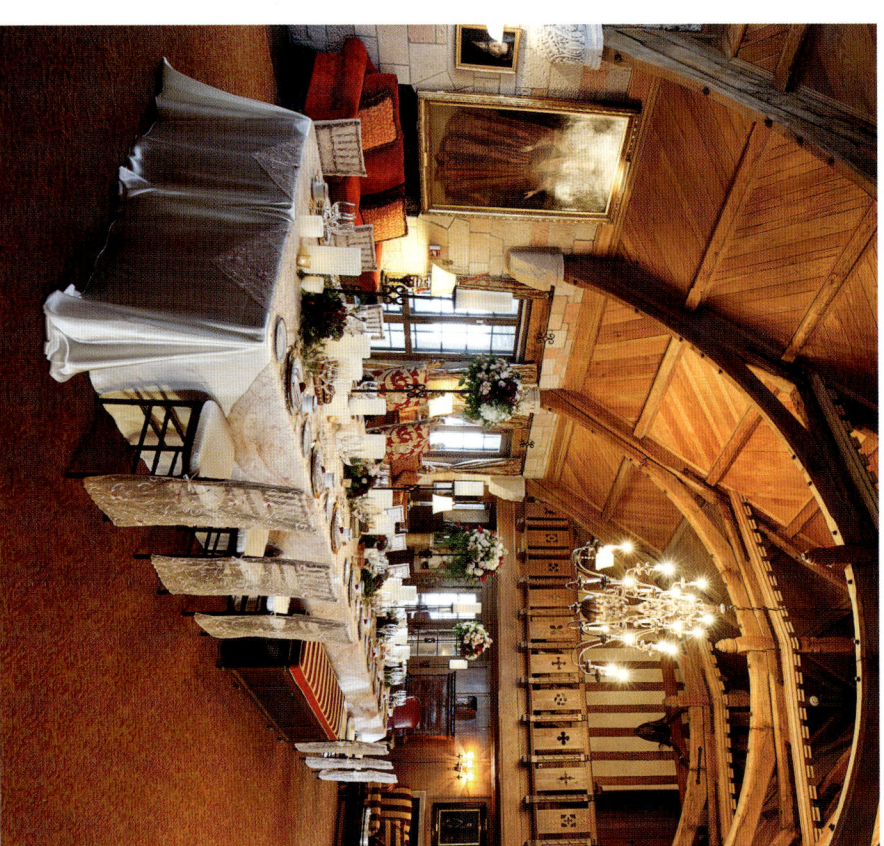

Photograph courtesy of Studio JK Photography, Joe Keum

"The right linens can transform a room from 'ordinary' to 'wow!'"

—Linda Bluhm

Right: Two napkins of different fabrics provide a stunning contrast for the peacock fold.

Facing page left: We unified each fabric's unique texture—quilted base cloth, delicately pleated mid-cloth, and an embroidered and beaded overlay—through the continuity of color.

Facing page top right: Mountain elegance exudes from the copper and green tones, beaded overlay, and chair covers.

Facing page bottom right: We draped the ivory charmeuse material elegantly on each corner of the table while the textured overlays and chair covers provided transition to the strong surroundings.

views

- ❖ Use fabrics in unique ways for lasting impressions.
- ❖ Fabrics and colors should complement the surroundings, not overwhelm them.
- ❖ Coordinating colors in linens, centerpieces, and china has a strong, cohesive presence.

LMD Productions

RODD METCALF

Rodd Metcalf has the rare ability to flatter a bride without saying a word. His signature blend of tone-perfecting, mood-altering lightscapes complement everyone from the mother of the bride to the best man in ways each had only dreamed possible. Through deft application of light and fabric, he creates ambience out of thin air, and his skill with a sewing machine means that drapes, scrims, sheers, and faux ceilings can be custom-sewn to match any planner's fantasy.

His ability to marry the visual and the tactile has helped Rodd become known as one of Colorado's most exciting event architects. For this reason, brides, grooms, and socialites who understand the transformative power of high-end fabric and indirect illumination flock to Rodd for his miraculous spatial metamorphoses and hands-on attention along the way. On the lead-up to any given event Rodd can be found, surrounded by a team of assistants and seamstresses, hand-smoothing fabrics and checking on the banks of whisper-silent generators that provide the electrical oomph his creations require.

Like the wizard behind the curtain, he is capable of drawing a room full of guests to attention with one dramatic, room-washing color shift. The most important moments, like the bride and groom's first dance, are signaled not with a tap on the microphone but with an eye-catching change in the color of the room. The effect is dazzling enough to silence 100 conversations in an instant yet elegant enough to appeal to Colorado's most discriminating hosts.

To accommodate the couple's request for vibrant shades of pink, blue, aqua, and orange, we bathed the whole room in rich color. The space took on a rosy glow as guests entered, then shifted to indigo for the first dance. When the parents took the floor for a waltz, we opted for flattering, golden tones which make everyone look fantastic. Finally, a vibrant teal encouraged everyone to get out on the dance floor.

Lighting Design & Décor | 195

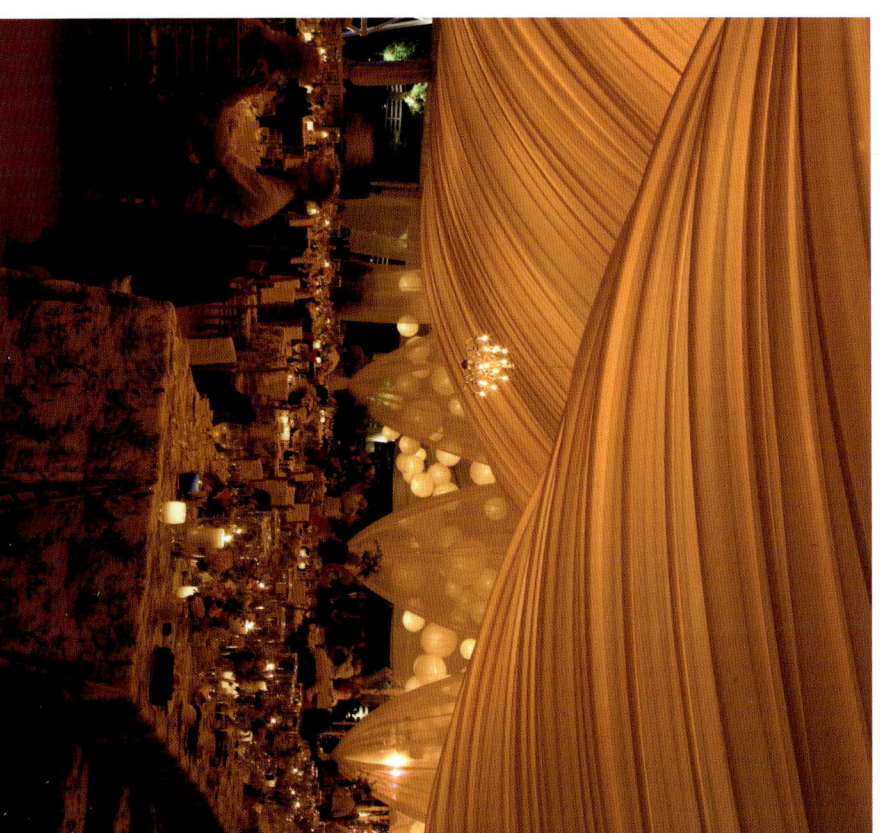

Photograph by Moments of Expression

"Open your party with golden or pink lighting so that everyone starts off looking beautiful. Wait until the dance floor opens to pump up the wilder colors."

—Rodd Metcalf

Right: For a wedding at the Four Seasons, the bride wanted everything to have just a hint of pink—nothing overwhelming and no changing colors. We directed pink uplighting at the base of the drape and the base of the huppah, even adding a trace of pink inside the chandelier. As a finishing touch, gentle spotlights on the bride and groom guarded against unflattering shadows.

Facing page top left: The Ritz-Carlton Bachelor Gulch in Beaver Creek is the ideal spot for an elegant, well-lit event. During dinner, guests glimpsed a glowing stand of Aspen trees through a curtain of sheer fabric. When the time came to dance, the sheers parted to reveal a dance floor surrounded by Aspen tress and bathed in rich, auroral light.

Facing page top right: To create an autumnal feel at a September wedding at Crooked Willow Farms in Larksburg, Colorado, we cozied up the walls with sunset colors and pin-spotted every centerpiece with LED light.

Facing page bottom: To create a soft, indirect ambience inside an enormous, ClearSpan tent, we designed an unbleached muslin liner—which itself took a week to set up—and clamped 70 fixtures to the beams above it. By directing the spots upward, we were able to reflect the light off the ceiling and back down through the muslin. The resulting illumination was inconspicuous and dreamlike.

views

If you want fantastic lighting, make sure the venue can support it. Often, high-end hotels can handle the electrical load but will charge extra for the power or the rigging clamps in the ceiling. When the bill comes, the couple ends up shell-shocked. Avoid the hassle up front by making sure there are no hidden charges.

SWANK STEMS

NICOLE IVERSON

Nicole Iverson, owner and creative force behind Swank Stems—Fine Floral Fashion, is an artist first and foremost. While her award-winning floral compositions are deferential of all elements and principles of design, she is quick to admit a penchant for color. Whether it is a kaleidoscopic assemblage of vibrant hues or a monochromatic display of muted tones, the end result is always a stunning spectacle of petal, leaf, and stem.

With an education in fine arts, a nearly decade-long career in the interior design industry, and a lifelong fascination and love of flowers, Nicole decided to change course and launch Swank Stems, a progressive floral design studio creating innovative décor solutions for the spectrum of life's celebrations. The career shift provided the perfect outlet for her artistic, entrepreneurial spirit and a much-needed emotional connection to her work.

Leveraging the indispensable insight she gained fashioning environments and experiences as an interior designer, Nicole is mindful of how her pieces harmonize with other elements and the overall aesthetic of an event. Whether a clear vision has been formulated or there is vetting yet to be done, Nicole collaborates with hosts to capture each one's unique style, whether whimsical, edgy, traditional, or avant-garde, to create exclusive floral sculptures. Her personal investment in the celebrations she has the honor of participating in is evident in the quality and execution of each and every design.

Successful collaboration with other professionals for consistency and cohesiveness throughout an event is essential. At the International Special Events Society Fantasy Table Design Competition, our team's overall motif was to present the details and finishes of a romantic, luxurious tablescape with a vintage aesthetic. We used a combination of hydrangea, hybrid roses, dahlias, mokara orchids, and stock and calla lilies for a sultry arrangement of warm plums and cool violets punctuated with splashes of fuchsia.

"Every cake has a story that is expressed in the details, flavors, and design."

—Janusz Zrodlowski

Right: For an *Alice in Wonderland*-themed wedding, I created several detailed drawings, as is my usual process, and the couple loved the 40-inch-tall stacked teacups and teapot. I made the top teacup from pastillage—a sugar-based dough that dries hard—so it could be kept as a memento.

Facing page left and top right: Other elements of the event, like the invitation, often inspire my creations. A boxed wedding invitation featuring a steampunk theme prompted a unique design with very intricate details that also blended well with the venue, a former factory. The event planner for a birthday celebration sent me the party's invitation, and we based our concept from there, adding uniquely shaped, vase-like tiers.

Facing page bottom right: The honoree—who was celebrating her 80th birthday—enjoyed all things fashion, so I designed the cake as the room's elegant showpiece with pulled sugar pieces on top. Fashion-themed cakes, like the vintage hat, surrounded the individual desserts.

views

A cake or dessert is not solely about the taste and the appearance. Of great importance is the construction, especially with fresh fruit or light mousse fillings, because you want the dessert to stay in the proper form throughout the event.

JS DESIGN
JULIE SANDUSKY

An invitation, by definition, is a formal request for a person's presence at an event. When crafted by Julie Sandusky of JS Design, however, an invitation is an exquisite work of art that conveys the mood, theme, and excitement of the upcoming occasion. It is a delicious hint at the experiences awaiting attendees, and Julie's impeccable eye for detail and fearless assembly of intriguing materials ensure that from the moment guests receive their invitations, they are enchanted.

JS Design was formed in 2003 as a creative outlet for Julie's exceptional talents. Enamored with paper products even as a child, Julie enjoyed an early career as an event planner and spent a year traveling the globe with Up With People before delving into the realm of stationery. Now she produces not only invitations but placecards, favors, gifts, and other unique items, all designed and created to reflect the vision of the event. All printing and bindery equipment is operated in-house, ensuring that the quality of letterpress, flat and screen-printed items never wavers.

Whether they've been contemplating their theme for years or would simply rather place their trust in her experience, Julie's clientele—which includes professional athletes, high-profile executives, and renowned organizations—always reach the same conclusion: this is the most memorable invitation they have ever seen.

I love creating products that expand the idea of what an invitation can be. By using quality papers, unusual ink colors, delicate lace, and graphic elements such as scrollwork, I created an invitation that was soft and elegant with a vintage, rustic edge.

With Much Joy

MRS. AND MRS. EDWARD M. DENNING
REQUEST THE PLEASURE OF YOUR COMPANY
AT THE MARRIAGE OF THEIR DAUGHTER

Marie AND *James*

SON OF MR. AND MRS. DAVID E. THOMAS
SATURDAY, THE TWENTY-SEVENTH OF JUNE
AT HALF PAST FOUR O'CLOCK IN THE AFTERNOON
CROOKED WILLOW FARMS
LARKSPUR, COLORADO

Reception to Follow

"Great invitations set the tone, and it's the details that make all the difference."
—Julie Sandusky

Right: Some weddings require a double dose of creativity. Printing the couple's logo on wood veneer gave a Ralph Lauren-inspired invitation the chic, understated flair the couple craved.

Facing page top left: Each design springs from the individual's personality and passion. One couple's love of tattoos translated into a design that was simultaneously bold, glamorous, and edgy, with the bride's orchid tattoos serving as inspiration for the invitation's background.

Facing page top right: A combination of hand-drawn calligraphy and high-quality materials results in an exquisite, handmade, boxed nvitation.

Facing page bottom left: Guests love receiving interactive invitations; imagine opening a box filled with jelly beans and containing a mini-puzzle that, when assembled, reveals the details of the event.

Facing page bottom right: A springtime invitation, designed for Beaver Creek Resort, called for letterpress printing on luxurious cotton paper that was then wrapped with a pale turquoise satin ribbon for a warm finishing touch.

views

Paper is a constant in the stationery world, but don't be afraid to experiment with more unusual materials. Lace, ribbon, fabric, and even wood veneer can help create a memorable impression, and may spark ideas for other ways to make your event one in a million.

SIGNED & SEALED BY STEPH
STEPHANIE ZAITZ

In this era of electronic communication, there is something remarkable about an exquisitely designed invitation being delivered to your door—it is personal, evocative, and intriguing. Stephanie Zaitz understands that invitations are meant to make a statement from the moment they are received. She forged her own niche in the high-end stationery market and earned a reputation for crafting stunning personalized stationery, invitations, and announcements for all of life's special celebrations. In fact, in 2010 and 2011, Stephanie's designs were given the prestigious ICON award for best invitation.

Merging her strong business acumen, creative talents, and extensive experience working for a trend-driven buying office at a high-end retailer, Stephanie launched Signed & Sealed by Steph in 2007. Working with a recherché collection of boutique stationery designers, Stephanie develops exclusive designs that artfully fuse a host's discriminating style with the latest fashion trends in paper. The ultimate custom design is echoed on all printed pieces to brand an event from save-the-dates to programs and placecards to thank you notes.

Eliciting excitement about an event starts with form and fashion. Employing a plethora of techniques, Stephanie molds each invitation to fit the host's personality and event theme. By incorporating vintage letterpress impressions, etched acrylic pieces, innovative layout concepts and packaging, or stylish motifs and embellishments, Stephanie transforms paper into a fabulous first impression, setting the tone for a festive, unforgettable event.

The bride's affinity for jewelry served as the inspiration for the escort cards, which we displayed atop piles of sparkling gems. The envelopes were secured with custom metal seals engraved with the bride and groom's monogram.

Printed Materials | 213

"Invitations generate buzz long before an event begins."
—Stephanie Zaitz

Right: Vintage elegance can only describe the one-of-a-kind wedding invitation consisting of three lush layers all artfully bound with a wide, double-faced silver ribbon.

Facing page: There are a plethora of sensational design ideas out there. My specialty is tailoring them to align with a host's sensibilities and style, creating something meaningful and deeply personal. Regardless of the overall motif, whether it is modern whimsy, environmentally minded, luxe couture, or simply elegant, we can help make a statement guests won't soon forget.

views

Invitations are the first glimpse guests have into a celebration. Clearly they serve a fundamental purpose of providing information, but more than that, they should make a statement, be reflective of the host, and set the tone for an event.

Capturing

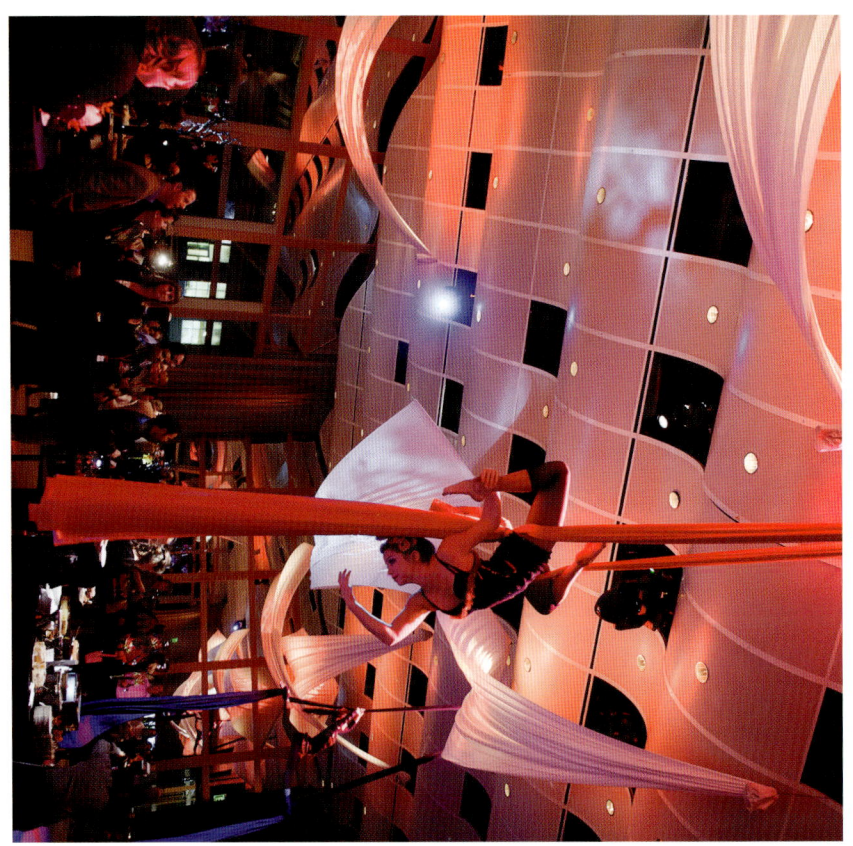

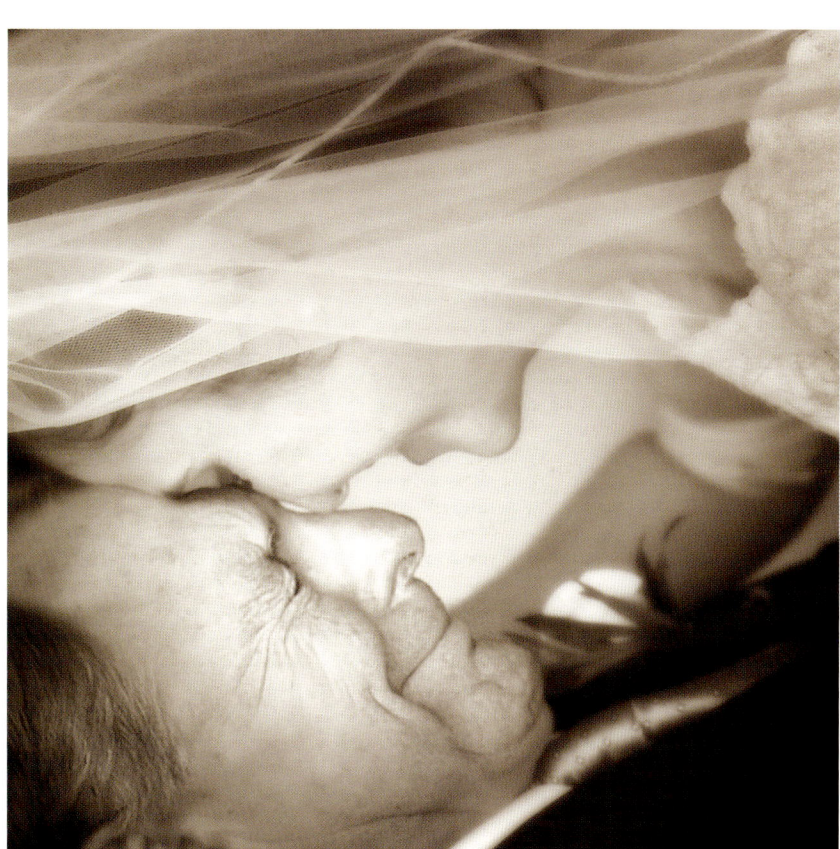

the Moment

Andrew Clark Photography

ANDREW CLARK

One of Andrew Clark's most cherished possessions is a photograph that was taken in 1904 of his great-grandfather. Opening a window into his family history, the photo reveals a wealth of knowledge, which bonds Andrew to that generation of his family heritage. The photo is, without a doubt, a family treasure.

That same connection between generations and the same level of emotion sparked by his family photo is exactly what Andrew strives to accomplish when taking photographs today. His focus on weddings—such huge milestones in the human race—has risen from that desire, and he could not think of a better way to spend his life than partnering with people on such a happy day.

Described as a destination wedding photojournalist, Andrew began his journey into art as a child enamored with color and expanded his horizons through an art scholarship, travels to more than two dozen countries, and photographic experience gained through several decades of creative practice. Countless subtle combinations of expression, perspective, color, light, and gesture are captured by Andrew in order to convey various emotions in stunning images. But even more important than Andrew's undisputed technical skills is his ability to adapt to any situation, whether the guest list is a who's who of high society or an intimate setting of close friends and family. Either way, the resulting art is a vivid, emotional story that will be passed down through generations.

In telling the bride and groom's story, I always include beautiful, heartwarming shots of the setting, like the spectacular La Casa Que Canta in Mexico. In many ways, the setting embodies their personalities and what's important to them.

"Photography is not just a career; it is my life. Even at the age of 100, I'll still be trying to perfect this wonderful art form."

—Andrew Clark

Top and bottom left: Artistic elements, whether adding a bit of forward motion or using black and white tones, can create incredible emotions that a standard shot might miss. Capturing the bride's beauty in a way that's unique to her in that moment is at the forefront of my mind. To combine these two ideas is a great challenge and is only achieved through natural, unposed photography.

Facing page: The surrounding light is always a large factor in what elements I focus on and what effects I add later. When the sun is setting, I'm able to capture a soft, romantic glow. In the blue tent during a rain delay, the tones were simply amazing and created an incredible backdrop.

Photograph by Andrew Clark Photography

Photograph by Andrew Clark Photography

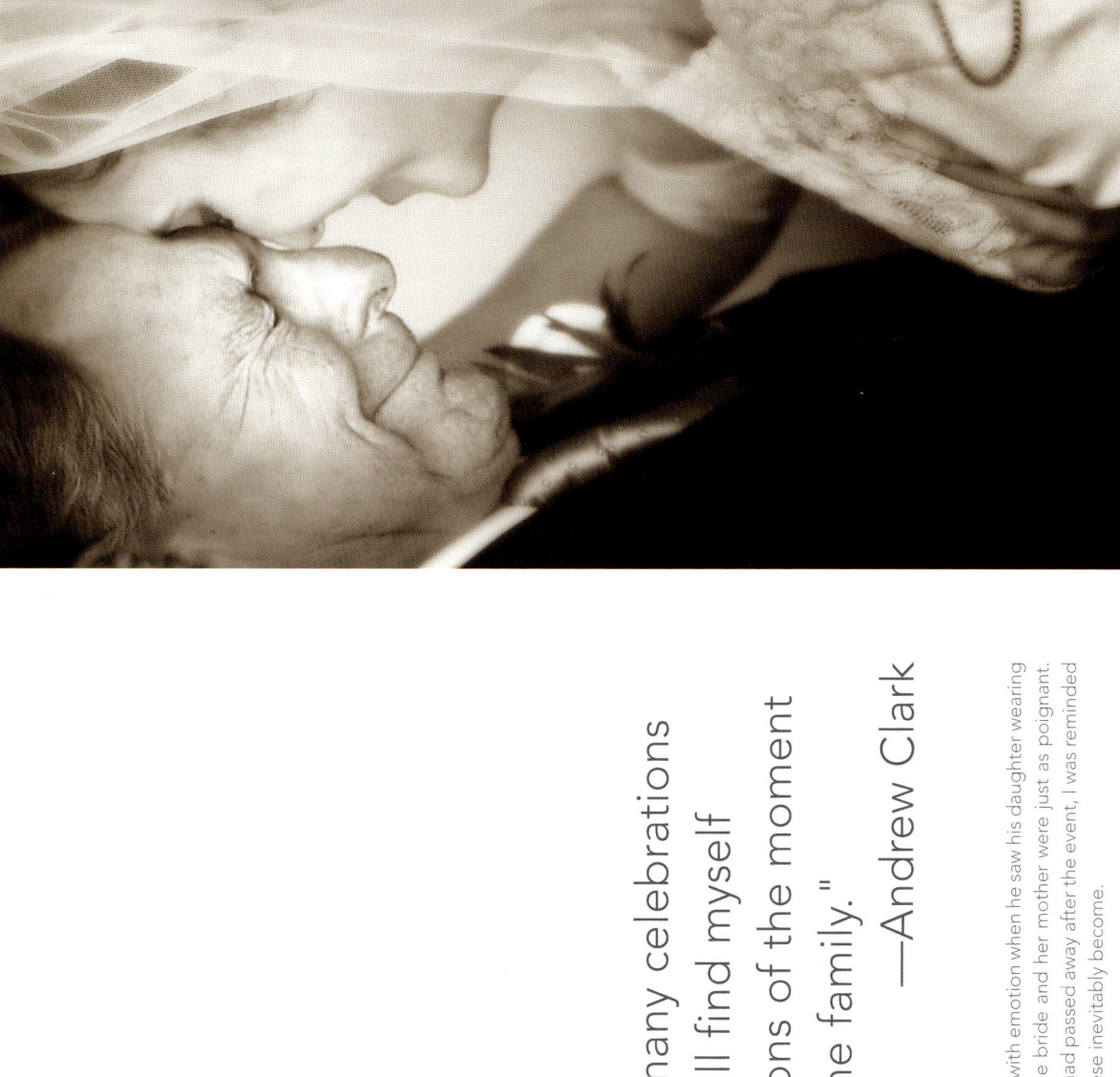

Photograph by Andrew Clark Photography

"No matter how many celebrations I've attended, I still find myself feeling the emotions of the moment right along with the family."
—Andrew Clark

Right: The father was simply overwhelmed with emotion when he saw his daughter wearing her mother's wedding dress. Images of the bride and her mother were just as poignant. When I found out that the bride's mother had passed away after the event, I was reminded again how important family photos like these inevitably become.

Facing page: Whether shooting the reception space for a multimillion dollar wedding or capturing the spontaneous exuberance of the newly wedded couple, it's always my goal to be in the moment so no detail or emotion is missed.

views

A photographer needs to have one of the most complex collections of skills on the planet. He or she must be technically flawless, able to inspire confidence, comfortable relating to every personality type, creative, and adept at working efficiently yet silently. It's the ultimate collaboration of creative artistry and technical expertise.

Frances Photography

FRANCES MARRON

A successful career in event and portrait photography may not have always been Frances Marron's goal, but that's only because she was too busy spending her formative years excelling at other pursuits. A lifelong dancer, Frances originally chose a path to pre-med to satisfy her technical tendencies, but found she missed having a creative outlet. After graduating from the University of Colorado and spending time in Fiji, she selected photography—the perfect amalgamation of science and art—as her life's direction. Training at the prestigious Brooks Institute of Photography, receiving Certified Professional Photographer status, and founding Frances Photography in 2001 have all prepared Frances for an occupation she now couldn't imagine her life without.

Equipped with the ability to instantly read people's emotions and adapt to their unique energies, Frances turns assignments into treasured friendships. What starts with a wedding often segues into maternity shoots, boudoir sessions, and family portraits. She believes that her images are meant to capture not only how someone looked on the special day, but how they felt, the energy that surrounded them, and the details that might otherwise fade from memory. Whether directing someone one-on-one or catching the perfect, spontaneous group shot, zeroing in on a particular facet of the décor or encapsulating the sweeping Colorado scenery into one image, Frances uses her logistical brain and artistic talent to tell the comprehensive story of a cherished occasion.

When you photograph still objects, you don't have to worry about someone's expression changing. This is where my science brain comes into play: I can take more time to set up my camera and determine the correct composition, as well as crop in the frame instead of later in my studio.

Photography by Frances Photography

"I shoot from the heart because I want to capture what people feel."
—Frances Marron

Photograph by Frances Photography

Above: A groom who was so in love with his bride had enough of posing and just couldn't resist kissing her for another second. A purely spontaneous, honest moment that just happened to have glorious light—sometimes you can't even plan what ends up being the best shot.

Facing page top: I love to shoot the details. Using a video light, which is a handheld continuous light source, I can direct where the shadows fall and don't have to rely on the unpredictability of a flash.

Facing page bottom: The first look for a bride and groom is such a special moment, because it's one of the few times during the day that they don't have an audience. When the bride is walking down the aisle, there are so many other things on her mind—don't trip, smile, hold the flowers correctly—that it's difficult to be fully in the moment of seeing her soon-to-be husband. Before all the craziness ensues, it's nice to snag a few minutes of nothing but tenderness and raw emotion. So they don't feel like I'm encroaching on their genuine moment, I shoot those types of images from 15 to 20 feet back with a long lens.

Photograph by Frances Photography

Photograph by Frances Photography

Photograph by Frances Photography

"A photograph is only as powerful as the story it tells. The story is in the emotion."
—Frances Marron

Right: Important elements from my technical background—analyzing light and composition, imagining foreground, the rule of thirds—come into play when I'm determining the texture and depth of field for a shot that encompasses the entire room.

Facing page: You always have to work with the energy of your subjects. An enthusiastic wedding party might result in a shot that's brimming with fun, while a more subdued couple may exude a romantic movie aura.

views

Only hire a photographer who you would want to be your friend. The best images come when everyone's personalities connect, and remember that whatever energy is in the air will be reflected in the photos. How the photographer makes you feel will show through, so make sure they make you feel comfortable and happy.

Studio JK
JOSEPH KEUM | JOYCE KEUM

A wedding is a momentous celebration for any couple. Planning often includes an overwhelming array of details: invitations, flowers, cake, decorations, and entertainment. But, undoubtedly, finding a skilled and creative photographer to document the day's priceless and fleeting moments is the most important detail of all. That is exactly what you get with Joseph and Joyce Keum, husband-and-wife team behind Studio JK, a progressive photography outfit specializing in preserving the nuances and candid emotions of upscale nuptials.

Capitalizing on backgrounds in photo editing and graphic design, and a combined 16 years of professional photographic experience, Joseph and Joyce believe that capturing a wedding beautifully is entirely dependent upon understanding the uniqueness of each couple. By taking the time to get to know a bride and groom long before the big day and to fully appreciate their precise vision, individual personalities, and passions, Joseph and Joyce become friends photographically recording a story, not strangers behind a lens.

Employing their "life in motion" technique, they let the day unfold in a natural, unassuming way. Working in tandem, with their distinct creative and dynamic perspectives, the duo blends documentary candor with artistic vision to capture the moment and create a photographic narrative. The end result is a collection of visually stunning images that are an authentic expression of the bride and groom—elegance and joy, love and beauty, tradition and whimsy, life and family, hopes and dreams.

The natural environment constantly inspires us—especially in Colorado. In some shots, we like to pull back and allow the couple to become secondary to the incredible natural scene around them. Snow-capped peaks, vibrant wildflowers, fiery sunsets, and turbulent clouds provide an organic canvas that is constantly changing and challenging us to be innovative and imaginative. Capturing the emotional connection between two people amid nature's chaos begets images that are evocative of the overwhelming love and beauty of the moment.

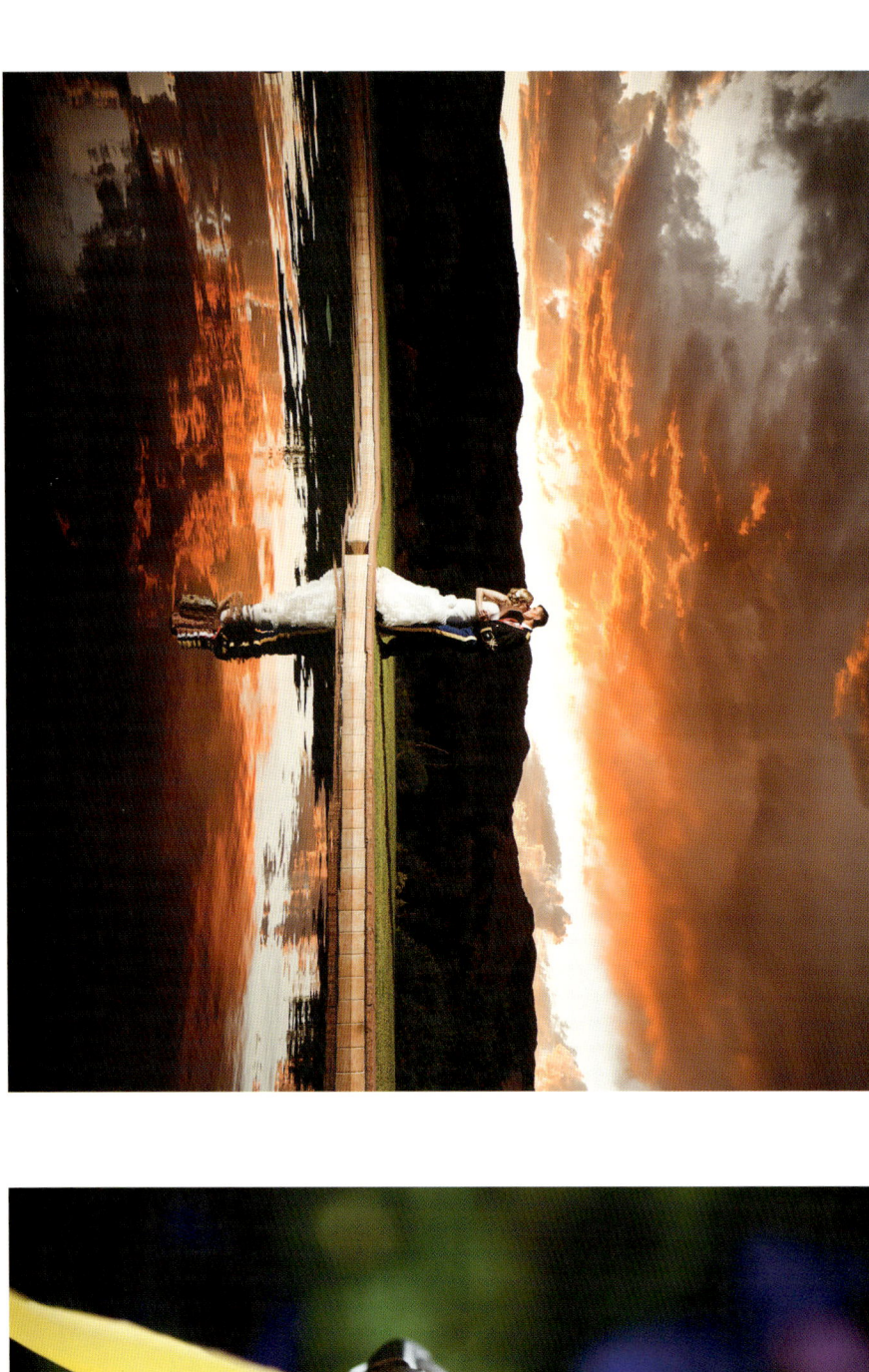

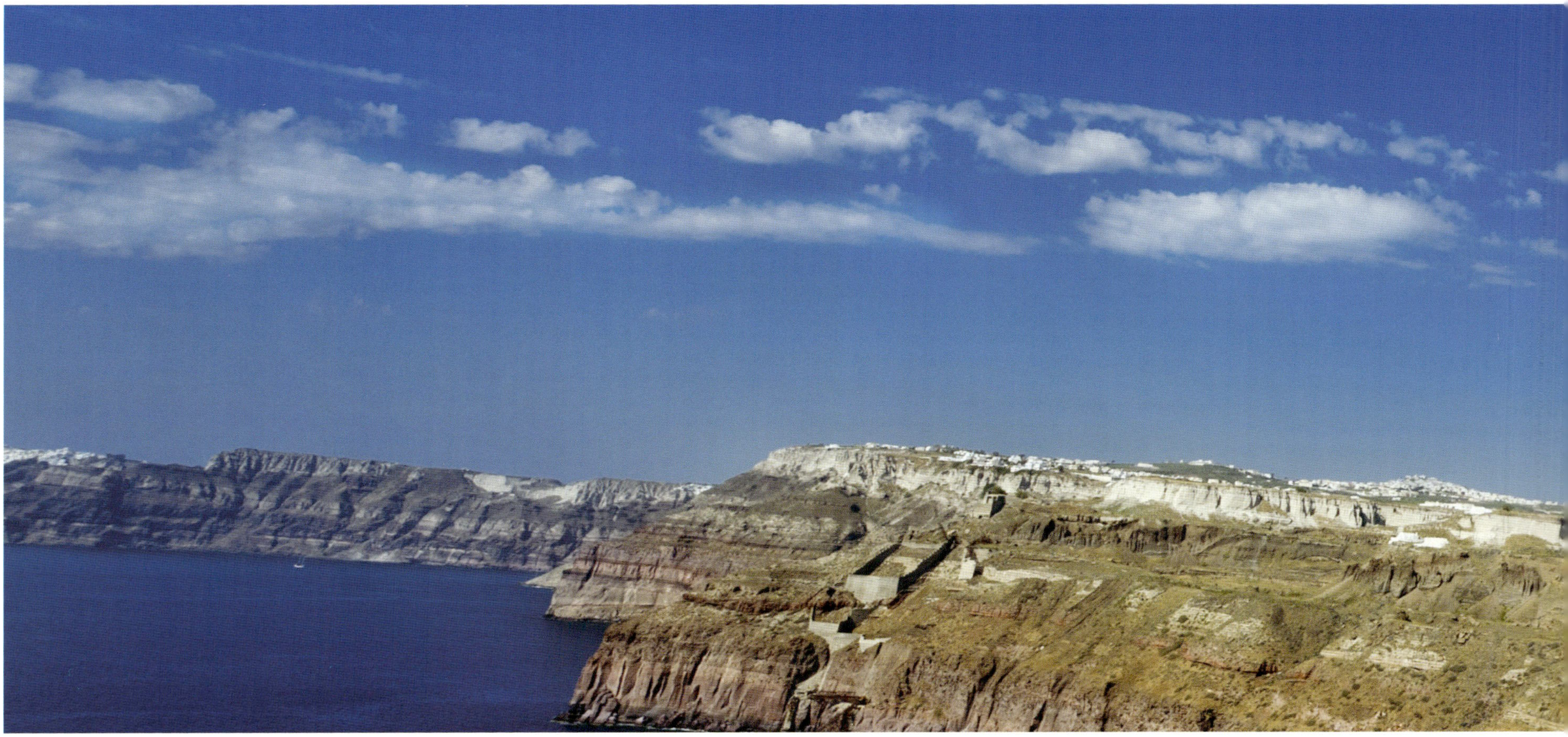
Photograph by Joyce Keum

Photograph by Joseph Keum

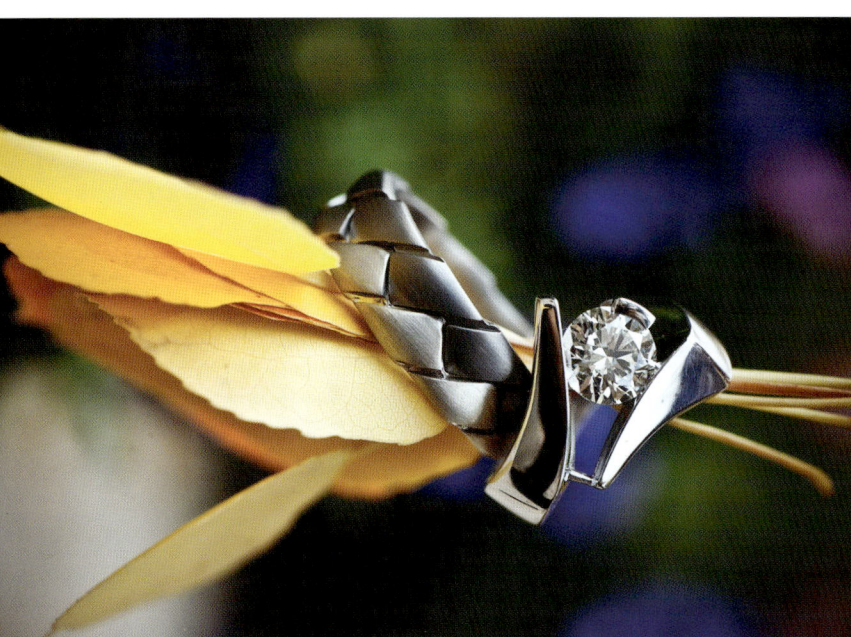

Photograph by Joseph Keum

Photograph by Joyce Keum

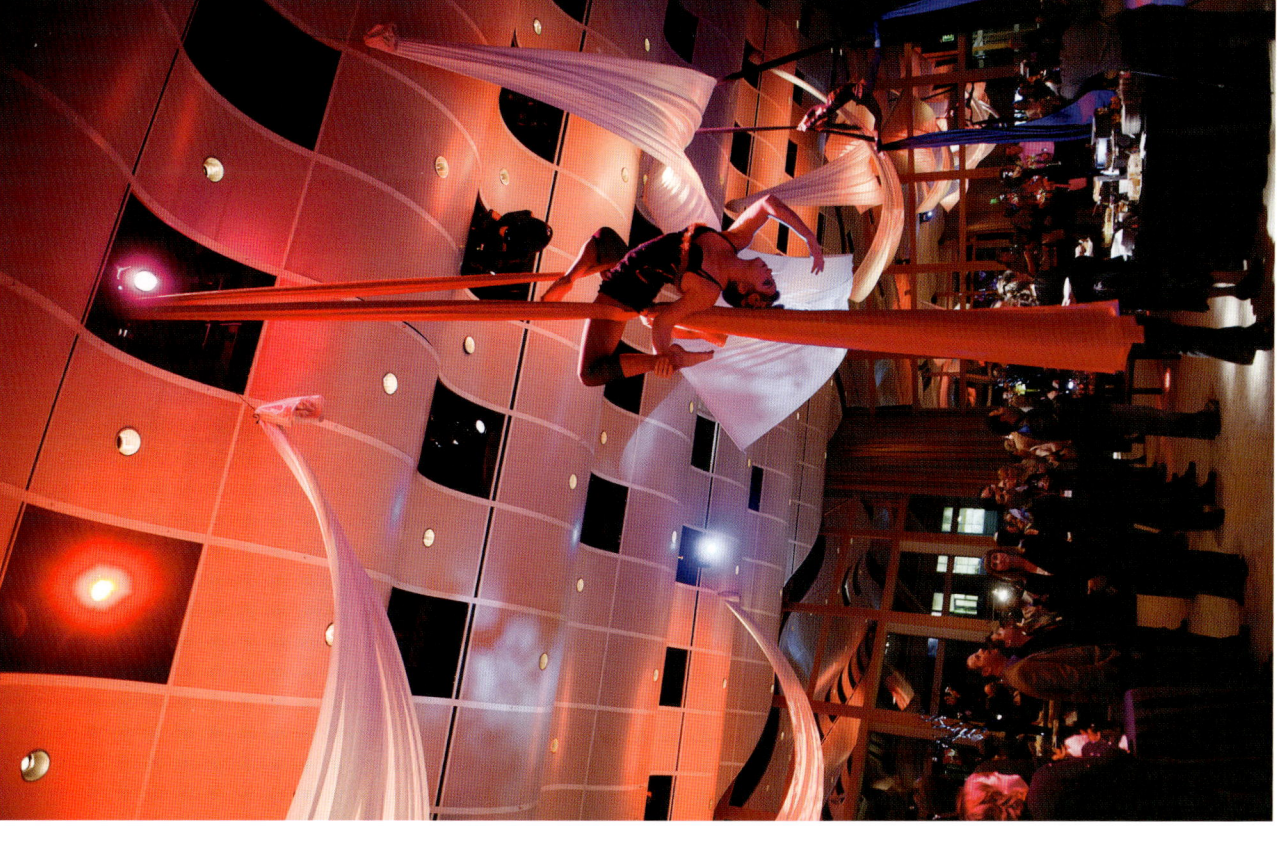

Photograph by Joyce Keum

"We don't just take photographs; we compose impactful images that capture the essence of our subjects and their surroundings."

—Joseph Keum

Photographs are experience captured. As memories fade, images will forever encapsulate a particular moment. Our approach to shooting a wedding and our overall style is a fusion of photographic methods—traditional, photojournalism, and artistic. By blending the three, we believe our images represent the true spirit of the moment.

views

After all the wedding preparations, the day is yours. Don't forget to enjoy it. Relax; be natural. It will absolutely come through in your photographs and make them that much more beautiful.

Autumn Burke Photography

AUTUMN BURKE

Located in the heart of Denver's historic Washington Park neighborhood, Autumn Burke Photography is a boutique studio that specializes in weddings and lifestyle portraiture. With a discerning eye for detail and a passion for telling the story, Autumn artistically captures the beauty, joy, and intimacy of life.

For Autumn, the draw of photography has always been about people, documenting authentic moments, and telling stories. The connections she develops are what keep the process continually creative and interesting. Every interaction through the lens is different, but the depth of emotions is a common thread throughout; a sense of love, family, romance, and joy permeates each of them. Whether that means capturing the silhouette of a family walking in a sunset or catching the sweet subtle gesture of the groom's hand resting on the bride's back, Autumn knows it's the little moments, often unexpected, that translate into the richest emotions.

Autumn exudes a passion for her work that is contagious. Her visual artistry combines with her technical expertise to create evocative imagery—images that catapult the viewer back to the emotion of the moment. With an eye for strong composition and a distinctive use of light and shadow, Autumn's photographs are unlike any other—she provides a unique vision that communicates the connection between her subjects and reflects the poignant moments that touch the heart.

I love depicting a moment in layers. From the bride and groom's embrace in the foreground to the guests and breathtaking décor in the background, layers add depth and dimension to a shot.

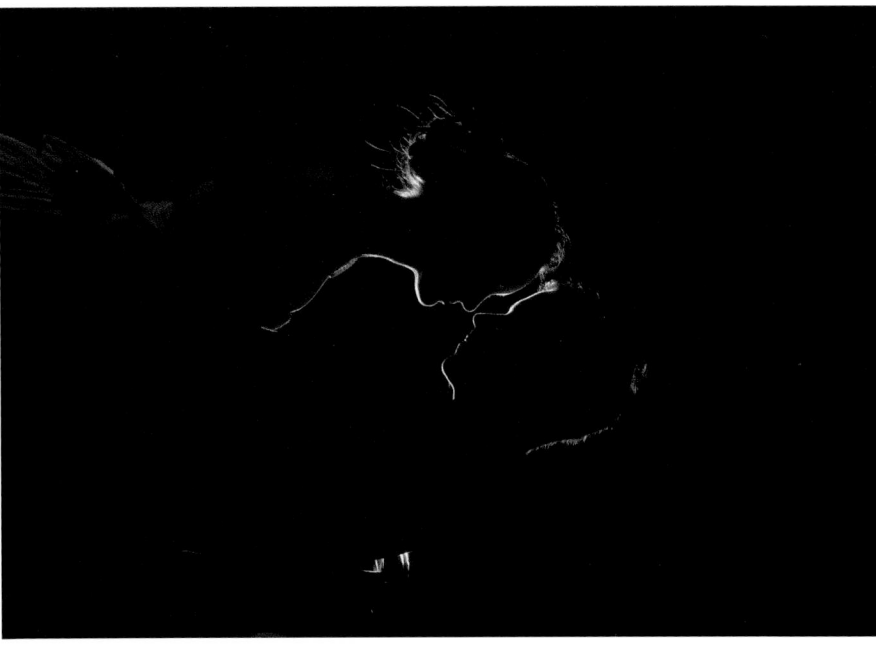

Photograph by Autumn Burke Photography

Photograph by Autumn Burke Photography

"Photography is all about light, and I love playing with the light to create compelling imagery that reflects the essence of the moment."
—Autumn Burke

Top right: Sometimes it's not about showing everything in a photo. The small details—ruffles of a bridal gown, a hand on a waist, wildflowers at the couple's feet—translate into an artistic representation of the shared emotions. It's not always about what you see in a photo, but what you know is being felt.

Bottom right: After months and months of careful planning and preparation, the wedding day often goes by in a whirlwind of excitement. Photographs of the venue provide a way to remember each exquisite detail. There are so many memories tied to a place that a simple image of a room will evoke emotions when looking at the photo years later.

Facing page top: If I'm going to tell the story of the day, I have to capture the entire mood of the event. Functions at the Seawell Grand Ballroom at The Denver Center for the Performing Arts are always beautifully lit and dramatic, which makes them such a delight to shoot. Through the proper use of lighting and composition, a sweeping shot of the room can convey the event's grand, sophisticated atmosphere.

Facing page bottom left: I'm not super-traditional, but I do love classic milestones—like a bride heading off to the wedding ceremony. The excitement on her face and the sense of elegance she exudes are things I want to be sure to convey, and the anticipation in her eyes tells you exactly how she's feeling.

Facing page bottom right: Light can be used to focus on a subject, or it can manipulate the shot so that everything else disappears. I love dramatic lighting—the interplay of light in a silhouette allows the rest of the world to disappear from the image, leaving just a suggestion of the people who are all that matter.

views

Find a photographer whose style speaks to you on an emotional level. You can give anyone a list of shots, but it's their vision that will translate into treasured images. Chemistry between the couple and photographer inspires trust on both ends and allows the photographer to be at their most creative.

BROXTONART
TRAVIS BROXTON

For Travis Broxton, photography is an artistic statement that mesmerizes the viewer. It's a visible record of the event that's distinctive and filled with honest emotion, which he captures and highlights through dynamic angles, bold colors, and dramatic cropping.

From the first moment Travis held a camera in his hands as a teenager, he felt something special. Originally a serious hobby, his passion blossomed as he displayed his photojournalistic, black-and-white street photography at Core New Art Space. Then when a friend and his soon-to-be bride requested he shoot their wedding, Travis found his true calling.

Travis throws out all agendas at an event, relying on the relationship he's built with the couple to allow the photos to truly represent the experiences of that day and the spontaneous moments of emotion. Even the "formal" session is not so formal but more a relaxed, efficient session to showcase the families' love and affection. Edgy, fashion-oriented, pushing the envelope, photojournalistic—these have all been used to describe Travis' work, which results in beautiful keepsakes that bring to light the love, joy, and passion of each moment on that big day.

During a beautiful sunset, we walked out to the edge of the cliff and I just encouraged the bride to be herself. I captured her in a moment of simply celebrating life, since she recently had almost died from a spider bite.

Photography | 241

Photograph by broxtonArt

"My number one goal is to make sure everyone feels extremely comfortable with me; that allows me to be in the midst of those precious moments without disturbing the scene."

—Travis Broxton

What separates those with a camera from true photographers is the ability to anticipate when something's going to happen. Shooting photojournalistic street images for nearly 25 years prior to capturing events gave me both a conscious and subconscious awareness of potential moments. I'm perpetually on alert, ready to sense where and when they'll occur.

views

Even with digital cameras, there's more to the art of photography than simply pressing a button. It's important to understand the rules of good design and imagery before attempting to break or bend them. When choosing a photographer, be sure to peruse their entire body of work, not just the best of the best shots, to really understand his or her capabilities.

Eric Stephenson Photography

ERIC STEPHENSON | MONI STEPHENSON

Eric Stephenson's life reads like the perfect resume. Each position builds upon his natural photography talent, enhancing skills that are invaluable for the events he and his wife, Moni, focus on today.

Eric's interest in photography began in high school and simply took off from there. His work as a custom printer improved his already meticulous eye, and his professional experience in New York City enhanced his creative and technical capabilities. Documentary work provided unparalleled experience in unobtrusively observing and capturing the action, while his days as the director of Denver Art Museum's photographic services department showcased his impressive lighting techniques.

All of these talents come together through the boutique studio that is known for its pairing of natural, photojournalistic shots with creative, almost fashion show-like images. An event's story is wonderfully memorialized as Eric and Moni capture the individual personalities, memorable moments, and sumptuous details that make the party special. An unprecedented level of preparation goes into every event, including an advance walk-through of the site to determine the best backgrounds, vantage points, and lighting techniques. Eric Stephenson Photography is the amalgamation of years of experience that leads to fresh, forward-looking images, obviously created by two people who have a passion for the important events that punctuate life.

We scouted The Ritz-Carlton Denver a few days before the event and knew the grand staircase would be a beautiful setting. By planning how we would light the area and visually rehearsing how we would achieve each shot, we were able to light and shoot from six different angles in only four minutes on the day of the celebration.

Photograph by Eric Stephenson Photography

Photograph by Eric Stephenson Photography

Photograph by Eric Stephenson Photography

Photograph by Eric Stephenson Photography

"A good image will have nice composition and technique, but a great image will also capture drama, emotion, or excitement."

—Eric Stephenson

Our goal is to simultaneously capture the day's story while also showing off the venue and the meticulous details that have been planned for months and months. The challenge comes in creating expressive images that achieve this goal quickly and unobtrusively. We have refined our lighting techniques over the years to make sure you'll never see harsh flash lighting in our photos because we want the images to reflect the natural beauty of the event.

views

For the most part, a beautiful venue and wonderful décor give the photographer a lot to work with. Be aware, though, that a room aglow in candlelight—which is stunning during the event itself—will require some tradeoffs in the images, so be sure to talk with your photographer about the lighting that will be used and what you can expect.

JARED WILSON PHOTOGRAPHY

JARED WILSON

One of photographer Jared Wilson's more unforgettable shoots was a destination wedding at a rather unconventional location. The bride and groom exchanged vows at St. Andrew's School in Middleton, Delaware, where the Academy Award-winning "Dead Poets Society" was filmed. But this self-admitted movie buff finds every ceremony, whether it is in Colorado or the Caribbean, more memorable than the next.

Growing up, the flash of a camera was a ubiquitous occurrence for Jared, whose father played the serious shutterbug of the family. Once he had a camera of his own and started shooting, Jared discovered it was a natural fit. In 2005, Jared took the leap, leaving a career in music ministry to pursue photography as a full-time profession.

Now his specialty is weddings, from engagement photos to last dance moments. Serious heart and passion direct Jared's work, as do the relationships he forms with his clientele and their families and friends. The results are emotionally charged photos that forever document a couple's love. He considers the genre the ultimate reward for an artist who craves the chance to capture a full range of sentiment, from anxiety to sheer ecstasy and everything in between. But wedding photography also allows him the fulfilling opportunity to create lifelong memories for a bride and groom. No wonder Jared's motto for his work has always been, "treasure this day forever."

The wedding reception at The Denver Center for the Performing Art's Seawell Grand Ballroom took an army of people to accomplish. The monochromatic tones and lush textures were jaw-dropping, and I wanted to capture every detail of the fabulous ambience.

Photography | 249

"My heart guides my photographs. It may seem unusual, but I often find myself crying during the father-daughter dance or the best man's speech."

—Jared Wilson

Right: The mix of peacock-themed reception tables and Art Deco-influenced ironwork at Denver's historic Oxford Hotel provided an interesting setting to show off an Alisa Benay gown.

Facing page top: I photographed the groom and his groomsmen underneath an overpass in Chicago, juxtaposing their elegant formality with the industrial edge of the city's underbelly.

Facing page bottom left: We found a Parisian-inspired courtyard about a block away from the reception venue. The red curtains in the background frame the bride beautifully; she wore one of the most amazing dresses I've ever seen.

Facing page bottom right: Both architects, the bride and groom were interested in a classically inspired yet artistic photo of their wedding party. The soaring columns and architectural detail of the Denver County Courthouse provided the ideal backdrop.

views

Wedding photos should be timeless expressions of a couple's love. I like to fuse a classical approach with a modern, fresh edge while avoiding any style or technique that may register as too trendy, perhaps losing its significance five or 50 years from now.

Lynda Hanshaw Photography

LYNDA HANSHAW

Plunging into the Solomon Sea with her camera to catch an off-beat bride grinning up from the blue depths below her—bouquet still in hand—Lynda Hanshaw of Lynda Hanshaw Photography knows no bounds when it comes to her work. As an international destination wedding, event, and portrait photographer, Lynda has braved the biting temperatures at the top of a snowy peak and even felt the wind whip through her hair on horseback to catch that perfect shot. Whether a bride needs a photographer to accompany her to the colorful streets of Costa Rica or new parents commission her to preserve the memories of their baby's baptism, Lynda is as much at home on ski slopes as in traditional celebration venues.

Trekking across the world, Lynda has captured some of life's most intriguing events through the lens of her camera. She has carried her camera to over 38 international locations and is a winner of the ICON Award for best photography. Lynda has also been recognized as one of the very select nominees for the International Special Event Society Esprit Award for best photography. From the grin of a stranger on the busy streets of China to the sparkling eyes of a Great Dane lounging on an ottoman, Lynda's photographs represent everything in life worth celebrating. Her images illuminate world cultures, commemorate the happiest day of a couple's life, and preserve emotions—including something as humble as the love between a preschooler and his canine best friend—for years to come.

The moments really worth capturing are those that are felt, not necessarily those preserved in a posed picture. Eyes express so much when a subject isn't thinking about how they should be sitting, where to look, or if their lipstick is straight.

Photograph by Lynda Hanshaw Photography

Photograph by Lynda Hanshaw Photography

"I always look for the spirit of the moment, but it's finding the spirit of the person I'm capturing that makes photography worth doing."
—Lynda Hanshaw

Right: There's so much humor to be found if you just look. Shooting the personality of a subject humanizes the experience.

Facing page: I shot my first wedding underwater in the Solomon Islands. While not every event calls for such extremes, the attention to detail is just as necessary when swimming with whale sharks as when shooting a traditional celebration. Natural light filtering past a building from above, towering décor pieces, or sweeping panoramic views of a room give photographs a sense of place. They preserve the moments that will elicit memories decades after the celebration ends.

views

Find a photographer willing to take risks and think outside the box. A diverse portfolio speaks volumes about a professional's diversity and her ability to capture what's unique about you and your event. When you love what you do, it shows.

WonderWorks Studios
STEVIE CRECELIUS

When celebrities set foot on Denver stages or large-scale public events are produced, photographer Stevie Crecelius is the professional sought out to capture those special moments. Whether shooting panoramic views of Denver landmarks or getting up close and personal at a wedding, the owner of WonderWorks Studios is known for her diversity.

A photographer in the Denver area since 2003, Stevie's easy-going, non-intrusive style is part of the reputation that precedes her. Pick up any literature about the Mile High City and chances are Stevie's photographs grace the pages. She has served as photographer for local hotels and restaurants, philanthropic auctions, and fashion events. Throughout her career, Stevie has captured the likes of Celine Dion and Cokie Roberts, who was in town to present at the Denver Scholarship Foundation fundraiser. WonderWorks Studios even won *Colorado Meetings + Events* magazine's best photography award in 2008, an achievement that speaks to her revered work. Stevie's eye for the details that matter means that the spirit of Denver is preserved for generations.

Motion shots, like fireworks exploding over the Denver City and County Building, convey the excitement of the festivities. The night sky provides a dynamic backdrop for grand celebration.

Photograph by WonderWorks Studios

"Photographs should have depth in their image and in their message."
—Stevie Crecelius

Everyone remembers the big stuff—who was onstage, what songs were sung, who caught the bouquet—but it's the little details that are worth preserving on film. They are the things that people miss in the moment but want to remember for a lifetime.

views

Photographers should have a niche they prefer working in, but they should be flexible enough to photograph any event, no matter the occasion or who's hosting.

Art of Celebration

COLORADO TEAM
ASSOCIATE PUBLISHER: Sharon Johnson
GRAPHIC DESIGNER: Lilian Oliveira
GRAPHIC DESIGNER: Jen Ray
EDITOR: Jennifer Nelson
EDITOR: Megan Winkler
PRODUCTION COORDINATOR: London Nielsen

HEADQUARTERS TEAM
PUBLISHER: Brian G. Carabet
PUBLISHER: John A. Shand
ART DIRECTOR: Emily A. Kattan
GRAPHIC DESIGNER: Lauren Schneider
MANAGING EDITOR: Lindsey Wilson
EDITOR: Nicole Pearce
EDITOR: Sarah Reiss
MANAGING PRODUCTION COORDINATOR: Kristy Randall
TRAFFIC SUPERVISOR: Drea Williams
DEVELOPMENT & DISTRIBUTION SPECIALIST: Rosalie Z. Wilson
ADMINISTRATIVE COORDINATOR: Amanda Mathers
ADMINISTRATIVE ASSISTANT: Aubrey Grunewald

PANACHE PARTNERS, LLC
CORPORATE HEADQUARTERS
1424 GABLES COURT
PLANO, TX 75075
469.246.6060
WWW.PANACHE.COM

INDEX

A Beautiful Memory............56
Kathy Vaughan
Boulder, CO
303.499.0959
www.abeautifulmemory.com

Affair with Flair............26
Leslie Heins
77 Charlou Circle
Cherry Hills Village, CO 80111
303.770.2200
www.affairwithflair.com

Amy Toltz-Miller Special Events............36
Amy Toltz-Miller
11673 East Berry Avenue
Englewood, CO 80111
303.589.4381
www.amytoltzmiller.com

Andrew Clark Photography............218
Andrew Clark
1481 South Gaylord Street
Denver, CO 80210
303.831.9090
www.andrewclarkphotography.com

The Aspen Branch............180
Beth Gill
309A Aspen Business Center
Aspen, CO 81611
970.925.3791
www.aspenbranch.com

Aspen Meadows Resort............138
Doug Crawford
845 Meadows Road
Aspen, CO 81611
970.544.7850
www.aspenmeadows.com

Autumn Burke Photography............236
Autumn Burke
616 East Kentucky Avenue
Denver, CO 80209
720.344.0710
www.autumnburke.com

Bethel Party Rentals............186
Martin Herrera
Maria Herrera
5396 County Road 154
Glenwood Springs, CO 81601
970.947.9700
www.bethelpartyrentals.com

broxtonArt............240
Centennial, CO
303.475.3456
877.298.7935

Calluna Events............64
Heather Dwight
4129 Amber Street
Boulder, CO 80304
303.443.4617
www.callunaevents.com

Creative Events and Occasions............46
Alisa Zapiler
201 Steele Street, 2nd Floor
Denver, CO 80206
720.231.8999
www.creativeeventsandoccasions.com

Della Terra Mountain Chateau............132
3501 Fall River Road
Estes Park, CO 80517
970.586.2501
www.dellaterramountainchateau.com

DesignWorks by Dave and Mike............160
David Squires
Michael Roffino
3869 Steele Street, Suite D
Denver, CO 80205
720.941.7440
www.designworksevents.com

Elegant Bakery............204
Janusz Zrodlowski
3278 South Wadsworth Boulevard, Suite 3
Lakewood, CO 80227
303.322.7708
www.elegantbakery.com

Eric Stephenson Photography............244
Eric Stephenson
Moni Stephenson
3686 Akron Street
Denver, CO 80238
303.596.7141
www.stephensonweddings.com

Faye Gardenswartz............72
Denver, CO
303.377.3472

Frances Photography............224
Frances Marron
13739 West 85th Drive, Suite B
Arvada, CO 80005
303.424.3800
www.francesphotography.com

Frosted Pink Weddings............80
Kelly Karli
PO Box 4234
Eagle, CO 81631
970.701.4157
www.frostedpinkweddings.com

Jared Wilson Photography............248
Jared Wilson
4705 West 107th Drive
Westminster, CO 80031
303.916.6409
www.jaredwilsonphotography.com

John Tobey Event Design............96
John Tobey
1620 Pennsylvania Street, Suite 2A
Denver, CO 80203
303.830.0889
www.jtobey.com

JS Design............208
Julie Sandusky
4340 East Kentucky Avenue, Suite 121
Glendale, CO 80246
303.484.1771
www.jsdesigncustom.com

JW Marriott Denver Cherry Creek............142
150 Clayton Lane
Denver, CO 80206
303.316.2700
www.jwmarriottdenver.com

Kelli Kindel Events, Inc.............102
Kelli Kindel
PO Box 370075
Denver, CO 80237
303.584.9191
www.kellikindelevents.com

Linens Unlimited............190
Linda Bluhm
4225 West 107th Drive
Westminster, CO 80031
303.463.6600
www.linensunlimited.net

The Little Nell............146
675 East Durant Avenue
Aspen, CO 81611
970.920.6322
www.thelittlenell.com

LMD Productions............194
Rodd Metcalf
PO Box 351919
Westminster, CO 80035
303.487.4444
www.lmdproductions.com

Lynda Hanshaw Photography............252
Lynda Hanshaw
175 Beaver Lane
Evergreen, CO 80439
303.674.6526
www.lyndahanshaw.com

Newberry Brothers 172
Paula Newberry-Arnold
201 Garfield Street
Denver, CO 80206
303.322.0443
www.newberrybrothers.com

Palazzo Verdi 150
6363 South Fiddlers Green Circle
Greenwood Village, CO 80111
303.763.1973
www.palazzoverdi.com

Puttin' on the Rizz 108
Richard W. Rizzo
1483 South Columbine Street
Denver, CO 80210
303.807.3857
www.puttinontherizz.com

Sanctuary 120
Brad Thompson
7549 Daniels Park Road
Sedalia, CO 80135
720.259.0972
www.sanctuarygolfcourse.com

Seawell Grand Ballroom 154
Dawn Williams
1101 13th Street
Denver, CO 80204
303.572.4466
www.denvercenterevents.org

Signed & Sealed by Steph 212
Stephanie Zaitz
559 Madison Street
Denver, CO 80206
303.955.4249
www.signedandsealedbysteph.com

Special Events Design and Calligraphy 88
Walli Richardson
3131 East Alameda Avenue, Unit 501
Denver, CO 80209
303.725.5740
www.wallirichardsonevents.com

Studio JK 230
Joseph Keum
Joyce Keum
www.studiojk.com

Swank Stems Fine—Floral Fashion 198
Nicole Iverson
720.982.9639
www.swankstems.com

Table 6 Productions 14
Heather Allen
135 South Ivy Street
Denver, CO 80224
303.956.8566
www.table6productions.com

WM Events 114
William Fogler
767 Trabert Avenue NW
Atlanta, GA 30318
678.251.6363
www.wmevents.com

WonderWorks Studios 256
Stevie Crecelius
8200 South Quebec Street
Englewood, CO 80112
303.789.5222
www.wonderworksstudios.com

THE PANACHE COLLECTION

Dream Homes Series
An Exclusive Showcase of the Finest Architects, Designers and Builders

Carolinas
Chicago
Coastal California
Colorado
Deserts
Florida
Georgia
Los Angeles
Metro New York
Michigan
Minnesota
New England
New Jersey
Northern California
Ohio & Pennsylvania
Pacific Northwest
Philadelphia
South Florida
Southwest
Tennessee
Texas
Toronto
Washington, D.C.

Art of Celebration Series
Inspiration and Ideas from Top Event Professionals

Chicago & the Greater Midwest
Colorado
Georgia
New England
New York
Northern California
South Florida
Southern California
Southern Style
Southwest
Toronto
Washington, D.C.

Experience Series
The Most Interesting Attractions, Hotels, Restaurants, and Shops

Austin & the Hill Country
Boston
British Columbia
Chicago
Southeast
Southern California
Twin Cities

Weddings Series
Captivating Destinations and Exceptional Resources Introduced by the Finest Event Planners

Southern California

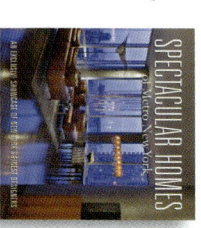

Spectacular Homes Series
An Exclusive Showcase of the Finest Interior Designers

California
Carolinas
Chicago
Colorado
Florida
Georgia
Heartland
London
Michigan
Minnesota
New England
Metro New York
Ohio & Pennsylvania
Pacific Northwest
Philadelphia
South Florida
Southwest
Tennessee
Texas
Toronto
Washington, D.C.
Western Canada

City by Design Series
An Architectural Perspective

Atlanta
Charlotte
Chicago
Dallas
Denver
New York
Orlando
Phoenix
San Francisco
Texas

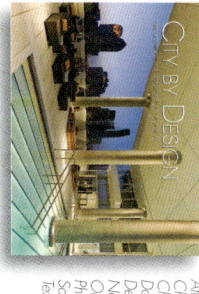

Interiors Series
Leading Designers Reveal Their Most Brilliant Spaces

Florida
Midwest
New York
Southeast
Washington, D.C.

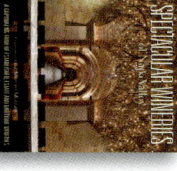

Specialty Titles
The Finest in Unique Luxury Lifestyle Publications

21st Century Homes
Cloth and Culture: Couture Creations of Ruth E. Funk
Distinguished Inns of North America
Dolls Etcetera
Extraordinary Homes California
Geoffrey Bradfield Ex Arte
Into the Earth: A Wine Cave Renaissance
Luxurious Interiors
Napa Valley Iconic Wineries
Shades of Green Tennessee
Spectacular Hotels
Spectacular Restaurants of Texas
Visions of Design

Perspectives on Design Series
Design Philosophies Expressed by Leading Professionals

California
Carolinas
Chicago
Colorado
Florida
Georgia
Great Lakes
London
Minnesota
New England
New York
Pacific Northwest
South Florida
Southwest
Toronto
Western Canada

Spectacular Wineries Series
A Captivating Tour of Established, Estate and Boutique Wineries

California's Central Coast
Napa Valley
New York
Ontario
Sonoma County
Texas
Washington

Spectacular Golf Series
The Most Scenic and Challenging Golf Holes

Arizona
Colorado
Ontario
Pacific Northwest
Southeast
Texas
Western Canada

Panache Books App
Inspiration at Your Fingertips

Download the Panache Books app in the iTunes Store to access select Panache Partners publications. Each book offers inspiration at your fingertips.

Panache Partners, LLC   1424 Gables Court   Plano, Texas 75075   469.246.6060   www.panache.com